BEYONCÉ
ONE OF ONE

HISTORY LESSONS,
LOVE LETTERS,
AND AFFIRMATIONS
FROM A
CULTURAL
ICON

ANTONIA JADE KING

BEACON PRESS
BOSTON

Beacon Press
24 Farnsworth Street
Boston, Massachusetts
www.beacon.org

Beacon Press books
are published under the auspices of
the Unitarian Universalist Association of Congregations.

Printed in the United States of America

29 28 27 26   8 7 6 5 4 3 2 1

This book is printed on acid-free paper that meets the uncoated paper ANSI/NISO specifications for permanence as revised in 1992.

Text design by BookMatters

Library of Congress Cataloging-in-Publication Data

Names: King, Antonia Jade author

Title: Beyoncé—one of one : history lessons, love letters, and affirmations from a cultural icon / Antonia Jade King.

Description: Boston : Beacon Press, [2026] | Includes bibliographical references and index. | Summary: "With a deep appreciation for Beyoncé's oeuvre and a commitment to highlighting the power of Black, Brown, and queer voices, King brings a unique perspective to this examination of Beyoncé's impact and growing legacy"—Provided by publisher.

Identifiers: LCCN 2026024427 (print) | LCCN 2026024428 (ebook) | ISBN 9780807022504 hardcover | ISBN 9780807022511 ebook

Subjects: LCSH: Beyoncé, 1981–Criticism and interpretation | Beyoncé, 1981—Influence | Singers—United States | Women singers—United States

Classification: LCC ML420.K675 K54 2026 (print) | LCC ML420.K675 (ebook) | DDC 782.42164092 [B]—dc23/eng/20260529

LC record available at https://lccn.loc.gov/2026024427

LC ebook record available at https://lccn.loc.gov/2026024428

The authorized representative in the EU for product safety and compliance is Easy Access System Europe 16879218, Mustamäe tee 50, 10621 Tallinn, Estonia: http://beacon.org/eu-contact.

For my wife,
the only thing I am sure about in this world.
Thanks for giving meaning to the music.

And for Silé Edwards.
This one's ours.

CONTENTS

ACT III: WHY HER HARMONIES WERE MY FIRST THERAPY

ACT IV: ENCORE—WHY BEYONCÉ'S MUSIC AND PERFORMANCES STAY WITH US

INTRODUCTION

I am going to start by introducing myself with a memory. I often lament and worry about my lack of childhood memories, but I do have a few very vivid ones. In this one I am ten and sitting cross-legged in my very purple bedroom in my very white hometown. I've just finished writing the kind of angsty and woefully unedited poetry that you write when you're ten and feel everything so deeply that emotions reach your bones. I then did what I would recommend everyone with too many feelings do: I listened to music. I'm from a generation where how we listened to music seemed to change every year. My portable CD player turned into an iPod, and that turned into an iPod Nano, which became an MP3 converter on my phone, and so on and so forth. So, I don't recall exactly how I was listening to music, but I know what I was listening to: Beyoncé's *Dangerously in Love* album. My favorite singer from my favorite girl band had gone solo, and I was following her career the best way I could before the advent of social media. All this space she took up, sonically and visually, was unlike anything I had heard or seen. Even at the age of ten, I saw images all around me telling me to shrink. But there she was—all big vocals, big curls, and big attitude. I remember listening to her music and willing myself to grow. In this memory, I am sitting cross-legged on a lilac carpet and falling even more in love with Beyoncé Giselle Knowles and by extension myself. In this memory, I made a subconscious choice to be a Beyoncé fan for life, and I hope that, by the end of this book, you will see that commitment has gone much deeper than screaming until my voice is hoarse.

As I aged and this love morphed into a deeper and more complicated appreciation for her as an artist, I became skilled at bringing Beyoncé into pretty much every conversation I have. My personal love for her music, and the fact that I am blessed to have many Black and queer friends, means I find myself discussing her a lot. These conversations are sometimes with people who share this love but often they are not. As such, I find myself justifying my love for her as often as I find myself conversing with fellow fans. The explanations I give for my admiration change frequently. During the first decade of the 2000s I would have probably mentioned her outfits, and after her release of *Lemonade* I would have discussed the themes she has explored and her visual output. However, despite the fact that the nuances and details of my answers may have changed, I always speak to the confidence I gain from her music. It might be the radicalism of simply seeing Black womanhood represented on the biggest stages in the world, or perhaps it's her lyrics or vocals, but something about her music improves my posture, mood, and confidence. The more I started talking about Beyoncé, the more I realized I am not alone in this. Her fandom, the Beyhive, is a proselytizing religion, after all. A friend of mine wore her natural hair for the first time to see Beyoncé's Formation World Tour, and another sent a picture of her newly bright pink bedroom with the caption "to the left" to our group chat to let us know she had finally left an unhealthy relationship. I believe the true power of Beyoncé's music lies in these personal highlights, in my elongated posture after a concert, and in the stadium lighting reflecting on my friend's curls. That's what this book is for me, an exploration of how Beyoncé has given us these moments, and that's why I started it with a memory.

More than simply admiring her talent or artistry, which would of course be valid, fans of Beyoncé have a deeper connection to her music. In today's cultural landscape, music serves as a powerful tool for expression, empowerment, and social commentary. Among the countless artists, Beyoncé constantly stands out for her unparalleled talent but also more recently for the profound impact her music has had on marginalized communities and Black women specifically. Those who are often excluded from center stage can see a reflection of themselves in her while she discusses issues that matter to them in a language they understand. It is for these reasons that I have formed friendships through the sole purpose of seeing Beyoncé, talking about Beyoncé, and saving money so I can see Beyoncé again. Popular culture holds so much weight and power, and now is the time to analyze Beyoncé's work with the depth of understanding it deserves. This book seeks to provide a deep dive into why her songs resonate specifically with underrepresented communities and the messages of empowerment and affirmations Beyoncé has chosen to channel through her music, lyrics, and visuals. Since the 1990s Beyoncé's songs have felt like love letters to the historically unloved, and through this book I hope to explain why and just how important those love letters are.

Before we delve into the themes in detail, I want to give a whistle-stop tour of her studio albums that trace a remarkable evolution in sound, storytelling, and cultural impact, each marking a new chapter in her artistic journey. Girl power is a part of the foundation of Beyoncé's career—after all she rose to fame in one of the most successful girl groups of all time. Even though there were controversies and reports of favoritism within Destiny's Child, all the girls were record breakers and cultural innovators. So, after a sometimes messy but always dramatic journey in 2001, Beyoncé Giselle Knowles and her fellow bandmates from Destiny's Child sang proudly about being "bootylicious" and how the world was not ready for their bodies (or the proverbial jelly). As well as "Bootylicious" being a pop anthem, the girls introduced a new word into the public lexicon (and the dictionary) with this song while celebrating a curvy body type that was not yet embraced by the mainstream media.[1] After numerous award-winning albums with the group, they all explored solo pursuits, and Beyoncé's debut solo studio album *Dangerously in Love* provided the blueprint for "going solo." This album gave us the catchy "Crazy in Love," which reached number one on Billboard Hot 100, as well as hits such as "Dangerously in Love 2," "Me, Myself and I," and "Baby Boy." I may have only been a kid at the time her first solo album was released, but no one could tell me that these emotional heartbreak ballads were not directly relevant to my experience. With its release, it was already apparent that she is something special. Her talent was always undeniable, but as she explored solo pursuits we saw more of her creative vision and determination to take pop and R & B music somewhere else entirely. *Dangerously in Love* was not just an album; it was a statement of intent, and she was already exploring themes of empowerment while making chart-toppers. As "Crazy in Love" opens, Beyoncé asked us if we were ready. We were not.

B'Day, her second studio album, released in 2006, drew upon sounds from the 1970s and 1980s funk genre, as well as R & B and pop influences inspired by her role in the film adaptation of the musical *Dreamgirls*. She used live instrumentation to accompany her vocals, and this combined with the range of funk, pop, and hip-hop influences resulted in an album that wasn't just triple platinum but so authentically Beyoncé and unique. As artists develop and grow, many must leave their old work behind, or at least distance themselves from it. This is not the case with any of Beyoncé's early work—songs such as "Irreplaceable," "Upgrade U," and "Déjà Vu" were popular when they were released in 2006 and have absolutely stood the test of time. Two decades later, during her COWBOY CARTER Tour, she performed "Crazy in Love," and her daughter Blue Ivy danced to "Déjà Vu." These early songs absolutely fit right next to her recent work because, just to be clear, she has always been excellent.

Her second solo album, *I Am... Sasha Fierce*, released in 2008, was a dual album to represent the contrast between her true self and her alter ego, whom she famously calls Sasha Fierce. Beyoncé has often spoken about how she harnesses Sasha to perform on stage, and this was fans' first formal introduction to her. The first disk is the ballad-heavy *I Am*, containing slow- and mid-tempo pop and R & B sounds. The second disk, *Sasha Fierce*, focuses on more up-tempo songs with Europop and electropop elements that took more risks.[2] The mix of sounds and personalities on the album create something that is again so unique. It was a perfect combination of sounds we had come to love and expect from Beyoncé, as well as an introduction to the different side of her.

In 2011 Beyoncé claimed that girls ran the world and showed us exactly how with her fourth studio album, aptly named *4*, which, as the Hive well knows, is her favorite number. This release importantly coincided with her father, Mathew Knowles, no longer acting as her manager and represented a change in her sound and artistic output. Beyoncé revealed that she made this album after taking a well-earned break to travel and spend time with herself and her family. She describes the album as a culmination of everything she learned during her year of travelling and time off.[3] This album truly does resemble the journey to self-discovery she describes and contains a mix of ballads such as "1+1" and "Love on Top," which are still loved among Beyoncé's ever-growing discography. It's a much more intimate album than her previous work, and I would argue that Beyoncé has cleverly and intentionally revealed more of herself with each album.

In 2013 she forever changed the way artists release music when she dropped her self-titled visual album with no promotion at all on a Friday evening. It is her most honest (and sexual) album to date, littered with electronic and soul sounds. Beyoncé had recently become a mother before its release, and her self-titled album provides rare glimpses into the life of this ultra-private star and in my opinion began the best four-album run of any artist in history. As a visual album, meaning the tracks were accompanied by a film, the videos that compile it were fundamental to understanding the music's lyrics and sounds. I personally cannot hear "Drunk in Love" without thinking of the iconic black-and-white footage of her on a beach. Of course, this increasingly sexual album drew critique, but Beyoncé was quick to remind listeners (with a song) that she is a grown woman. She also offers classic songs such as "Pretty Hurts" that critique the very nature of fame itself. The maturity that her motherhood brought is heard in every beat on this album. The attention to detail was and still is something to behold.

Her career has always been a masterclass in pop music, but Beyoncé's songs are far from vapid pop hits. Themes of feminism and sexual empowerment have been present in her music since her career began in Destiny's Child. From "Bootylicious" to "Freakum Dress," Black womanhood in all its complicated glory has always been front and center of Beyoncé's discography. She often receives critique for what some believe are her neutral or passive politics and for her extreme wealth. These criticisms are valid. However, I see fame as a tool that should and can be used to promote progress. It is also fair to say that Beyoncé has become more overtly political in her work, especially with her recent albums. Her music is where she makes her arguments heard and tells us who she is. She increasingly starts conversations, innovates, and empowers the unempowered through her music, visuals, and performances. Art does not exist in a vacuum, nor did it fall out of a coconut tree; it exists only in the context it is being consumed. Black women have historically been shamed for embracing their sexuality outside of the male gaze. Beyoncé breaks these patterns and the status quo by giving us increasingly "grown" and sexual visuals with her self-titled album and songs rich with innuendo such as "Ego" and "Rocket."

Not only does she explore gender dynamics and sexist double standards; Beyoncé's music has increasingly sought to hold a mirror to the American racial hierarchy. Arguably the culmination of this increasingly political Beyoncé is her second visual album,

Lemonade. Lemonade represented a shift sonically and thematically in her discography, serving as a statement of her intent. The visuals for the lead single "Formation" show her on top of a sinking New Orleans Police car in reference to the horrific tragedy of Hurricane Katrina, which disproportionately affected Black Americans living in the area. In 2016 I sat on my friend's floor watching as the sinking police car became gradually submerged in New Orleans floodwater and a young Black child danced in front of police officers, who were dressed in full riot gear. When Adele won the 2016 Grammy Award for Album of the Year, she dedicated the award to Beyoncé. Beyoncé's *Lemonade* was also nominated for Album of the Year, but Adele ultimately (and controversially) took home the Grammy. In her acceptance speech, which was entirely about Beyoncé, Adele called her the artist of our lifetime. What was more important about this speech in my opinion is that Adele specifically thanked Beyoncé on behalf of her Black friends.[4] Adele described how Beyoncé's music made her Black friends feel able to stand up for themselves. In that moment it was abundantly clear how much Beyoncé, and her discography, mean to so many Black women. To call her simply a pop star or celebrity does not do justice to the power, inspiration, and joy so many of us have harvested from her work over the last twenty years.

In 2023 she hung a rainbow disco ball in stadiums across the world and filled her stages with Black and brown queer and trans folks and ball culture as she toured her seventh studio album *RENAISSANCE*. She released *RENAISSANCE* during the COVID-19 pandemic, and it was an album of escapism through celebrating a club era where people sought community and freedom through dance music and Black queer culture. The album sounds like a DJ mix with seamless transitions from song to song and blends disco and house music while paying homage to the Black pioneers of the genres. In my opinion, *RENAISSANCE* is an ode to queer creativity. It is also, and perhaps more importantly, an ode to queer joy and freedom. With the tour she provided a safe, fun, and free space for queer people and worked with many queer artists on this album. In doing so she reclaimed genres of music created by Black queer people that have since been whitewashed and made us dance in the process.

With *RENAISSANCE* marketed as the first of three acts, in 2024 we finally found out what act 2 was after much speculation from the dedicated Beyhive. Beyoncé, never one for understated announcements, posed on a horse holding the American flag to announce that she was releasing a country album. While today, country music is associated with all-American white Southerners, historically the genre was pioneered by Black Americans, who are now often excluded from participating. Beyoncé is a native of Houston, Texas, by way of family from Louisiana and Alabama, but she is not exempt from this exclusion, as shown through the dismissal she received while performing at the Country Music Association Awards with the Chicks. Through the release of *RENAISSANCE* and crafting a fully country album, Beyoncé is reclaiming Black genres of music. What these moments and albums all have in common is that they are so much more than pieces of popular culture; they are some of the few reflections Black women and queer people have been allowed to see of themselves. Despite Beyoncé meeting critique for being quiet on many current and crucial issues, in her art she has become increasingly politically explicit with her latest albums such as *Lemonade* and *BLACK IS KING*. Alongside these developments her art has also continued to evolve in terms of its quality and scope. She consistently raises the bar for herself and others in terms of what her art is saying and the art itself. She is the biggest star in the world with countless award-winning chart-toppers, but her work is so much deeper than the accolades she has received for it. Her music is more than the craftsmanship and skill of her vocals and performances; it's the themes she explores.

Yes, Beyoncé has made me stand taller, but she has also made me cry many times and in several ways. Sometimes I cry because she's artfully articulated the pain of love; other times I cry because she's dominated the biggest stage of the world to pay respect to the Black Panther Party. To be a Beyoncé fan (or member of the Beyhive) is to be constantly fed and surprised. Every new genre she tackles, every album that I haven't mentioned in this introduction, every new medium she explores, every tour video and social media post, she handles with grace and excellence. The journey of Beyoncé's career is a long one and has seen her consistently change and elevate. For these reasons, I am truly of the belief that Beyoncé is a grossly underrated artist. However, when I say this, people give me an odd look and to some extent I understand this side-eye. Her awards are many, and her fans are vocal to say the least. This combination of factors, combined with the quiet yet omnipresent way she chooses to handle her fame, leads to Beyoncé seeming like (and being) the biggest name on the planet. And yet, all the fame and awards cannot do justice to what so many of us have taken from her career. The songs *are* phenomenal, but so are the love lessons and affirmations in everything she does.

So, when people ask me why I like Beyoncé, I speak about her continued dominance of the music industry, her being the greatest living entertainer and bending genres to her will. I speak of her being the first Black woman to headline Coachella and of the *Lemonade* film visuals shot on the site of the Madewood Plantation House. Sometimes I speak of hearing "Single Ladies" or "Run the World (Girls)" for the first time and feeling the true divinity of femininity in every note. All of this is true, and I have an immense respect for her as a craftswoman, but ultimately the real reason I am a fan is because of the impact her music has had on me personally. It may be a selfish answer, but I love Beyoncé for everything she has given me, for every moment her music has given me the permission to dance or cry and has made me feel seen while doing so.

ACT I

YOU READY?
WHAT THE WORLD MISSED IN BEYONCÉ'S FIRST ACT

BEYONCÉ, KELLY, MICHELLE, THE SUPER BOWL, AND SISTERHOOD

When Beyoncé headlined the Super Bowl in 2013, a moment many of us had been waiting for, she invited her former bandmates Kelly Rowland and Michelle Williams to perform alongside her.[1] After Beyoncé sang through a selection of her own hits, she launched into the introduction to the Destiny's Child hit "Bootylicious." When Kelly's and Michelle's personalized introductions from the song played, they popped out from underneath the stage. All three women were wearing black, looking like the accomplished superstars they are, and we all let out a collective scream (at least my friends and I did). After "Bootylicious," they performed the classics such "Independent Women Part 1" along with Beyoncé's solo hit "Single Ladies" (complete with the choreography from the music video). The moment was brilliantly executed and in keeping with the tradition of inviting feature artists on stage during the Super Bowl performance, but it also took us fans back to the start of her career. Beyoncé, at *one* of the heights of her career, brought out women who had traveled the journey with her, her sisters. To understand the gravity of that moment and why I screamed at the top of my lungs when Kelly and

Michelle popped out from the floor, you must understand the history of Destiny's Child.

Destiny's Child has been referred to as an R & B icon, having sold over sixty million records worldwide. Despite being so young when they first took the stage, they created music that had so much to say about girlhood, coming of age, bodies, and love. Their work remains relevant and loved today and has people begging for a reunion tour. Formed in the early 1990s, the group was known originally as Girl's Tyme. Based in Houston, Texas, Girl's Tyme initially consisted of six young members aged eleven and twelve: Beyoncé Knowles, Kelly Rowland, LaTavia Roberson, Támar Davis, and Nikki and Nina Taylor. In 1993 after attracting the interest of music producer Arne Frager in California, the group debuted on *Star Search*, a popular talent television show at the time. After Girl's Tyme lost the competition to a male group called Skeleton Crew, Beyoncé's father, Mathew Knowles, stepped in to manage the group and changed the lineup. These changes resulted in Davis and the Taylor sisters leaving the group and the addition LeToya Luckett. The girls performed locally around Houston, building their skills as performers and developing new material.

Under the name Destiny's Child, the group signed a recording contract with the Elektra Records label but was unfortunately dropped before an album was released. Despite the different iterations, the group maintained a recognizable sound. In 1998 the girls released their debut and self-titled album, a neo soul-inspired body of work with thirteen tracks. While I love this album, it did not achieve the success of their subsequent record breakers and it peaked at number sixty-seven on the Billboard chart but certainly intrigued audiences.[2] Then, in 1999, they released their second album *The Writing's on the Wall.* In comparison to their debut, the commercial success of *The Writing's on the Wall* catapulted the group into mainstream popularity. This album boasted a slew of hit songs including "Bills, Bills, Bills," "Say My Name," and "Jumpin', Jumpin'." The album redefined the image of female empowerment in pop music with the messages of feminism, solidarity, and empowerment. "Bug a Boo," a personal favorite, subverted the expectation that women should do anything to keep a man. Instead, the girls had us all signing about cutting a man off when he challenges your peace and constantly calls your phone, even those of us who were too young to have a phone.

A key part of the album is the interludes that seamlessly take us from song to song and are also expertly crafted. Playing off the theme of the Ten Commandments, the interludes are worded like biblical instructions but are about dumping your man. The interludes talk about financial freedom, toxic relationships, and sexual expression while mimicking Bible passages. All these brilliant aspects of the album meant that *The Writing's on the Wall* emerged unscathed from the tabloid press and the changing band lineups to become one of the best-selling R & B albums of all time. Despite many of the band members being only seventeen when the album was released, Destiny's Child cultivated a feminist message that stood out amid the saccharine girl-pop and heartbroken ballads of their contemporaries. The album was focused on everything women are and what they deserve. While the songs were catchy and radio-friendly, the focal point was the intricate harmonies that set Destiny's Child apart in a crowded R & B girl-group scene. The album also marked a shift in R & B, which now incorporated elements of pop, soul, and hip-hop, and helped Destiny's Child navigate a competitive industry with their distinct sound and fresh approach to production.

Just before the release of the "Say My Name" music video, Luckett and Roberson split with the management, believing Kelly and Beyoncé were favored artistically and financially. In 2001 they were replaced by Michelle Williams and Farah Franklin (who unfortunately was only in the band for five months.) However, despite the drama and controversies, these new additions solidified the group's future and sound. Three years after the release of *The Writings on The Wall* and with the revamped lineup of three members, Destiny's Child returned to the studio and in 2001 released *Survivor*. This was the group's third album, which reached the number one spot on the Billboard 200 chart. There were many challenges during this era of the band, not just the departure of Roberson and Luckett but also the legal battle over the group's name and the media's portrayal of these changes. The album represented their resilience in the face of these challenges and public scrutiny with empowerment anthems. The self-assured titular song "Survivor" became an anthem for women overcoming obstacles. This track, along with others like "Bootylicious," became symbolic of women's independence and confidence. Simply put, "Survivor" was a movement and mood. The three band members—Beyoncé Knowles, Kelly Rowland, and Michelle Williams—would make the defining image of Destiny's Child. Their fashion, style, and public personas became symbols of empowerment for young women, particularly Black women. Three of the album's songs—"Bootylicious," "Independent Women Part 1," and "Survivor"—made it into the top three singles on the Billboard charts in the United States. The trio also won the 2002 Grammy Award for Best R & B Performance by a Duo or Group with Vocals for "Survivor." The album was an undeniable success internationally, racking up notable sales in Australia and Europe.

There are so many qualities I love about every iteration of Destiny's Child, and I cannot neglect to mention the fashion and iconography. They went from wearing matching outfits in their early years to the bold, fashion-forward choices in their later years. Despite apparently finding it difficult to find fashion houses and labels willing to dress these curvy Black women, the group managed to become synonymous with high-fashion and cultural innovation. This, in no small part, was due to the clothes made by Beyoncé's mother, Tina Knowles, who also lovingly calls Kelly her bonus daughter. Their coordinated, yet personal, ensembles, including camouflage outfits of course, are an undeniable part of their legacy. In her autobiography, Tina describes how fashion labels initially rejected the girls' style and called it "homemade" and "too Black." However, these homemade and Black ensembles went on to influence early 2000s fashion—especially camouflage and rhinestones—eventually being copied by white artists.[3] Outside fashion, Destiny's Child continued to transcend boundaries with each album due to their unique sound, which sat somewhere in between R & B and mainstream pop. Their careers took off internationally, and Destiny's Child grew into a global brand with international tours and collaborations with global artists.

The journey may have been bumpy, but Destiny's Child went from a young group formed at an audition to having their own star on the Hollywood Walk of Fame.[4] They became one of the most influential female R & B groups of all time, launching the careers of Beyoncé and the other band members. This success was despite the tabloids' best efforts to exploit the so-called drama of the lineup changes.

But, all good things must come to an end, including Destiny's Child. The group, however, did not dramatically split; rather, the three band members took time to explore solo careers and interests before eventually parting ways. This meant that Beyoncé's burgeoning solo career started when Destiny's Child was still very much together. For example, her first solo studio album, *Dangerously in Love*, was released in 2003, years before the band split. She seamlessly handled the balancing act of being a part of the group while fanning the flames of her rising star power, including her ventures into acting and her debut solo album's success.

However, Beyoncé was not the only one making solo waves. The group's time apart allowed each member to explore their unique identities while still maintaining a bond of sisterhood. During the group's two-year hiatus, 2001–2003, Michelle Williams released her debut solo album *Heart to Yours*, which topped the US gospel album chart and became the best-selling gospel release of the year. Years later, in 2014, Beyoncé and Kelly featured on Michelle's song "Say Yes" from her album *Journey to Freedom*. Throughout Michelle's solo career, she's pursued acting on Broadway, in the theatres of London's West End, and on television. Kelly Rowland is also a powerhouse, with hits such as "Like This" and "Motivation" being standouts from her discography. Her debut studio album, *Simply Deep* in 2002, was also made during the group's hiatus. During this time, she recorded "Dilemma" with the rapper Nelly, which arguably became one of the biggest R & B hits of all time.[5] It has become common to use the phrase "the Beyoncé" to mean "the standout star," but what is so unique and amazing about Destiny's Child is the talent of every single band member and the sisterhood they still share. The songs we all love do not sound the same without Kelly's vocals and without Michelle taking us to the bridge.

Destiny's Child's messages of empowerment, friendship, loyalty, and independence still resonate in contemporary conversations about women's rights, race, and representation in the music industry. Thematic elements of empowerment in Destiny's Child's music mean that songs like "Say My Name" and "Survivor" connect with women across generations. They had a huge impact on pop culture, and Destiny's Child's discography has truly shaped the world of music and beyond. They have *all* had phenomenal and well-deserved careers, with their friendship enduring over the years. They continue to show up for each other, and not just for the Super Bowl. Kelly and Beyoncé attended Michelle's premiere of her starring role in the Broadway production of *Death Becomes Her*. They continued to collaborate musically by featuring on each other's songs, like Kelly's R & B song "You Changed." In October 2024, Kelly and Beyoncé attended a rally in support of then presidential candidate Kamala Harris, using their continued star power to try to get a Black women elected as president of the United States. This continued collaboration represents why we must all question and combat how the dynamics of Destiny's Child are so often used to get women to compete against each other. Many people will mindlessly reference wanting to be "the Beyoncé," when in fact the amazing body of work produced by all three band members should remind us of themes of sisterhood.

Even after their solo careers began, they continued to collaborate with artists from different genres and embrace new sounds like on their fifth and final album as a group, *Destiny Fulfilled*, which was released in 2004. This final bow of an album also gave us "Lose My Breath" and "Soldier," for which we are forever grateful, amen. Destiny's Child's final US tour was in 2005, before the band officially disbanded that same year in order to explore their solo adventures. However, their legacy in the music industry has never ended. Perhaps more importantly, their representation of strong, independent women in music helped to shape the narrative around female power and solidarity. Their music continues to inspire, thanks to the group's ability to adapt, innovate, and stay true to their roots.

The creative decisions and adaptability of Girl's Tyme allowed the group to transform into Destiny's Child, one of the best-selling girl groups of all time and one of the most influential musical acts in history. Even as the world moves forward, their legacy has shaped the modern music landscape and continues to empower listeners, especially women, on the global stage. From their humble beginnings, they truly became cultural icons. Destiny's Child's influence can also be seen in later girl groups and solo artists, particularly in terms of their unapologetic representation of women, their fusion of genres, and their expression of feminine sexuality. These themes of sisterhood certainly shaped Beyoncé's career and the way the public perceives her artistry, autonomy, and leadership. Empowerment and independence run through Destiny's Child's entire discography, and Beyoncé continues to take these themes with her into her solo work. Beyoncé's music connects with so many women, and that's because from the start of her career connecting with women has been at the center of what she did. So, the three-minute Super Bowl performance was more than just a reunion; it was a part of music history and a reclamation of sisterhood.

THE DREADFUL IRONY OF WOMEN'S SEXUALITY AS TOLD THROUGH BEYONCÉ'S DISCOGRAPHY

I think I was around sixteen when I first learned to look in the mirror and see shame in the reflection. At school one day, my friend had been told her shirt was too short. She'd had a growth spurt, and as such the hem of her school shirt did not quite reach the top of her trousers. At the time we were learning to find ourselves in our clothes. We all wore thick black eyeliner and rebellious bright pink tank-tops under our school shirts. Our head teacher, a woman (who went to my grandad's church), told my friend to cover up her midriff. The argument was that her sixteen-year-old midriff may, apparently, distract the male teachers. It would make them awkward, she said. They wouldn't know where to look. A male teacher stood solemnly behind her and nodded his agreement. Behind me in the corridor, a girl was being called a slut for not sleeping with a boy. Irony finds girls far too young, and I learned a lot that day. I learned that growing and maturing was something only boys got praised for, and that people aren't okay with women's bodies, and by extension I shouldn't be either. After that day I bought shorts to wear under my skirts as my clothes tended to ride up at the back. I would cross my arms in front of my chest in case my school uniform was just a bit too tight "there."

My single, feminist mother would ask me to think about how others may view my outfits and by extension me.

Our sexuality is barely known to us before other people start to define it for us. We can't learn our own bodies and how we want to show them before we must shrink ourselves to avoid making our teachers uncomfortable. These stories and these emotions aren't unique; in fact, they are far from it. As formative as these moments were, having spoken to friends I now realize these stories are "tame" compared to what so many women and girls go through. "Tame" though they may be, they taught me to lower my head. These expectations and this way of owning and shaming female sexuality follows us. It follows us into every job interview, into every date where we worry about not showing enough or showing too much. It follows us to the point where, even as I write this, I am still having to do work to define what my sexuality means to me outside of anyone else's gaze. That day, the day my friend learned to see her midriff through the eyes of her science teacher, I went home and listened to Beyoncé. I turned *Dangerously in Love* up so loud that my neighbors and my mum complained (my mum most of all). I was all teenage angst and wired headphones and that iPod Nano. I would play it everywhere. I would place my head on my school bus window and listen while my hair oil embarrassingly mixed with the condensation on the window. I would call my listening escapism, but it felt more grounded than that, more like a reclamation. With Beyoncé's music, I still felt men's eyes on me when I left the house, but not in my ears. For the three minutes and thirty seconds of the title song, I could bear witness to someone owning their sexuality while not being defined by it. Looking back, I am so grateful that before I had the words to articulate what made me feel small, I had these images and vocal riffs telling me it was okay to grow.

These experiences are my own, but the stereotypes and institutions that have been built to define, shame, and over-sexualize Black women are unfortunately universal. America, and the world more broadly, has never been okay with a Black woman's body, especially when that body does not exist for their gaze or dissection. Instead of allowing Black women to embrace their bodies with agency and on their terms, structures and stereotypes have been built to stop just that. The jezebel became a widely recognized stereotypical image used to define Black women during slavery, and it has persevered ever since. The jezebel has an insatiable appetite for sex; she is wild with desire and untamable. She is all lascivious hips and lips, but the most important thing to remember about the jezebel is she exists to rob us of our humanity. She is a victim of her own desire and an object of other people's. Far from being a stereotype that exists only on-screen, this image was and is actively used to justify white male sexual violence toward Black women. This and other stereotypes, and those who employ them, have sought to put Black women in boxes and to place another brick in the wall of dehumanization. Apparently enslaved women desired sexual relations with their oppressors, initiated them even. Apparently, you cannot rape an object.

The history of this stereotype is long and devastating, and *The Birth of a Nation* film, released in 1915, is a key part of this history. The film was originally entitled *The Clansman*, a title based on a book of the same name. The film supposedly tells the story of the redemption of the South by the Ku Klux Klan. Some stories are merely entertainment; this one wasn't. In the film white characters must protect their women from the savage Black man, who deserves to be lynched. The Black man was, of course, played by a white actor in blackface. The film was screened at the White House—the first film ever to be screened there—and given a seal of approval by President Woodrow Wilson. People called it a marvel, the most technically brilliant film ever made. People said the film highlighted the potential of American cinema—and they were not wrong.[1] Prominent white supremacists would later credit the film as aiding the revival of the KKK. Alongside its rewriting of history and apparently "brilliant potential," the film also introduced audiences to the character Lydia Brown, a Black woman played by a white woman named Mary Alden. Throughout the film Lydia uses her body and sexuality to tempt a white man into sin and peril. Lydia became aroused when she heard strong orders being given. Lydia, on the many occasions she did become aroused, would beat her breasts. Lydia achieved her aim of becoming a mistress and was a slave to desire. Lydia was, unfortunately, one of the most defining images of Black women that audiences were shown. Lydia was one of the first examples of the jezebel to hit American screens.

During the Jim Crow era, this violent obsession with Black women's bodies continued and morphed into something new yet old. White people would decorate their houses with ashtrays shaped like Black women's bodies, literally stubbing cigarettes out on their heads. Everyday items—postcards, sheet music, fishing lures, drinking glasses, and so forth—depicted naked or scantily dressed Black women. These images and the women they claimed to present lacked modesty and sexual restraint; they were the literal and figurative butt of the joke. Later, the Blaxploitation genre introduced audiences to the apparently "sexually liberated" Black whore. Black women were still sexual fodder, but in a different way. After all, nothing is more common in American cinema than the Black whore; even Halle Berry has had to play one in *Jungle Fever*.[2]

Decades after a film helped revive the KKK, President Ronald Reagan would use images of promiscuous "welfare queens" (Black women) to gather support for irradiating state support for the disenfranchised. From reviving the KKK to impacting federal policy, these stereotypes had wide consequences on- and off-screen. What is also crucial to understand is that these images and stereotypes have shifted and developed to stay relevant today; "the gold digger" and "the hoe" are just some examples. Very rarely is a woman allowed to define what her sexuality means for herself even if she is "allowed" to express it. Often, when images may appear to break the mold of these historical stereotypes, they are still showing Black women through the male gaze. You can see this in a camera shot that lingers on just one body part, therefore visually dismembering a dancer. You can see this in yet another music video where a man pours champagne down the back of an underpaid dancer. You can see this in the fact that we are supposed to be happy when the man does this because at least they hired a Black dancer. You can see this in the fact that nearly every Black actress has, at one point, played a prostitute. You don't have to look far to see that Black women's bodies are still so rarely their own.

Beyoncé's discography, including songs such as "Freakum Dress" and "Grown Woman," must be analyzed with this context in mind. Beyoncé has never been afraid to embrace her sexuality from a very early stage in her career. Destiny's Child embraced their curvy bodies in crop-tops and low-rise jeans and sung about how they needed a soldier, about how the world was not ready for their bodies. Arguably the world has never been ready for Black women's bodies. Their brand was all strong posture and fun, and their lyrics were explicit. For example, in "Soldier" they sing about how they want a man to keep their body screaming, never failing to set their own demands and sexual expectations. Though sexualization of Black women remains a problem in America, empowerment can be found in the way in which Beyoncé and Destiny's Child have always embraced their sexuality but on their own terms, something Beyoncé continues to do in her solo career. Beyoncé's lyrics often decenter men entirely by telling them literally and figuratively to sit down. There is a history of negative stereotypes being inflicted on Black women who embrace their sexuality in a public way, and she embraces this aspect of herself without fear and encourages others to do the same.

With her debut solo album *Dangerously in Love*, Beyoncé began her solo career by continuing to embrace her sexuality. The video for "Crazy in Love" for example shows a now iconic dance move that sees her turn her head to the side, shake her bum, and raise her hands above her head. Elsewhere in the video she lies on the floor and crawls in red heels and short denim shorts. The video for "Baby Boy," featuring Sean Paul, is also very sensual and sees her lie on a bed in a silver bikini.[3] Some may look at this video and argue that Beyoncé is being sexualized rather than liberated, particularly considering the relatively early stage in her career and especially as the video also sees Sean Paul fully clothed. However, her lyrics see her prioritize her pleasure, which is a theme that she has continued to explore in her work. Also, it is unsurprising in a debut album that the videos and the lyrics are sexual, especially when the album is *Dangerously in Love*, where Beyoncé collaborated with many male artists, including the incredibly sensual Luther Vandross.

In the early 2000s, videos showing women having champagne poured onto their bums and faceless strippers were common, and it is right to stay critical of this over-sexualization of women on-screen. However, even though Beyoncé was not engaging with sexuality with as much nuance as she does later in her career, what she was doing was still worlds away from these images. There was always empowerment in the way she owned her body and the amazing things it could do. The video for "Naughty Girl," perhaps the sexiest song on the album, sees her completely in control with lyrics about how she is feeling sexy and what she wants from her partner.[4] She states that she might take him home rather than being taken home herself, and she only dances with a man (a man who happens to be Usher) very briefly. She remains dominant in the choreography and lyrics while he is somewhat helpless. Even at this very early stage of her solo career Beyoncé embraces her sexuality in a way that placed her pleasure front and center. This is why in the video she kicks over her male co-star while wearing red heels and matching lipstick as she and her backup dancers remain in the spotlight. Throughout the video she dances but not for a man; in fact, he just sits and watches. Sexuality has always been a part of her music, and in an industry that often treats female sexuality as a commodity that exists for men, this is a feminist statement. From her very first solo album it was clear that these themes of empowerment and what she would later call feminism were there to stay.

In *B'Day*, her second studio album, released in 2006, Beyoncé engages with her sexuality in a similar way. The songs and choreography are sexual but again entirely on her terms. In the song "Kitty Kat," she tells her partner what her demands are. Her sexuality becomes a power that she decides to withhold until his behavior improves. "Green Light" similarly places her in a position of power where she is the one initiating sex. The videos for this album feature her more on her own rather than dancing for or on a man. In the video for "Green Light" she dances solo in black leather, and the video for "Get Me Bodied" features only women while she sings about finding a man in a club.[5] Her styling for this album centers on powerful stances and dark clothes and makeup. The lyrics and visuals work in harmony to portray her as in charge of her life and her sexuality. Men, if they feature in the videos, dance behind the women.

In "Freakum Dress" she explores how sexuality can be a source of power rather than something to hide from and feel shame about. She implores listeners to do what we need to do to feel good about ourselves and argues that our bodies are only our own to adorn as we please. She describes the joy in putting on a short and backless dress, explaining how she's been locked up in the house for too long.[6] Her partner in the song has, in contrast, been out. In this dynamic she explores how female sexuality is locked up, literally and figuratively, while men are praised for being out on the town. In the video men are not prepared and are almost helpless. This album also sees another feature with Jay-Z after the success of "Crazy in Love," "Déjà Vu," as well as a song with Bun B and Slim Thug, "Check on It." Even when she is with these powerhouses and male performers, she still dominates the interpersonal dynamics explored in the songs. For example, in "Check on It" she proudly "flaunts" what she has in a range of pink outfits, from a suit to a miniskirt. She then tells the men they can look but are not allowed to grab it.[7] Again, she is completely defining her own sexuality. In songs with Jay-Z and to some extent other male artists, her sexuality is deepened by connection rather than being defined by the men she is singing with. In the album she tells us all to continue to take charge of our own sexuality and not let any partner define it for us, either by locking us up or oversexualizing us.

Her 2008 album *I Am... Sasha Fierce* deals with sexuality in a different way. The lyrics are more subversive, and sexuality is discussed in the context of romantic relationships and long-term partnerships. These themes make sense when we also consider that this is her first album released after getting married, and afterward she embraced her sexuality differently. One of her most explicit songs on this album is "Ego."[8] "Ego" includes a hilarious and obvious double entendre as she sings about the large size of her partner's "ego." Rather than being a typically upbeat song, it is much slower. The video sees her with large curls and a backless silver leotard sometimes worn with a black oversized blazer, sometimes not. The lyrics include her asking her partner to open her body and stay in bed rather than go to work. Despite the song being about a heterosexual relationship (we assume), there are only women in the video. The powerful choreography and absence of men again create the impression that she is not sexualized; she's just sexy. The sexual lyrics within this album are within the context of romantic songs. The album is partly about multiple versions of self and how they can coexist, and the exploration of sexuality adds to this theme. These moments also demonstrate that sexuality is not in opposition to a person being emotionally open or to long-term partnerships; in fact, they serve each other. She does not have to give up her sexual desires or sexuality to have a relationship and be worthy of respect in that partnership. Despite the romantic and tender moments on the album, her sexuality remains entirely hers throughout the album as songs such as "Single Ladies" and "Diva" see her not only neglect men but deem them irrelevant. The result is an album that not only explores the beauty of female sexuality in romantic relationships but encourages us all to embrace every part of ourselves regardless of our romantic status.

The album *4*, released in 2011, is a more romantic and sensual album. Songs such as "Countdown," "End of Time," and "Love on Top" see Beyoncé express the joy of romantic love in upbeat and catchy chart-toppers whereas songs such as "1+1" and "I Miss You" intricately detail the pain of love. However, "Dance for You" features on the album and is overly sexual with lyrics describing being happy and secure in a relationship and dancing for your partner.[9] For the video she performs an almost striptease in stockings and wears big hair and a mini dress. While the visuals see Beyoncé and other nearly naked women dance for a man in a suit, the song is still about her desires and pleasure when dissected on a deeper level. If there is a power balance here to be interrogated, it is not in his favor. In fact, he is instructed to literally sit back and watch. Far from sex being something forced on her in the song, it is a way in which she decides to show her love for her partner and something that brings her a huge amount of joy. Notably this is the album in which "Run the World (Girls)" sits, where Beyoncé proudly proclaims that the entire world belongs to, and is run by, women. These songs combined tell the story of a woman who may dance for you if she wishes, but she will go back to running the world in the morning.

Late on a Thursday night in December 2013 Beyoncé released her most sexual album yet. *Beyoncé* unapologetically prioritizes sexual pleasure. This, crucially, is the first album she released after becoming a mother. On *Beyoncé*, she embraces her sexuality more overtly with a level of authority previously unseen. These aren't "wearing a backless dress in a club to get someone's attention" type of songs; these are songs describing a deeper sexual connection and talking about sex outright rather than alluding to it. "Blow," an upbeat dance track, is about pleasuring a woman. Given how many male artists will proudly exclaim that pleasuring a woman is irrelevant to their sexual endeavors, I think there is something radical in the way she demands it. "Partition" tells the story of a couple that are so in love and enamored with each other that they forgo their plans to have sex in a car. This car is a private limo—of course. These songs fit perfectly in an album that also explores feminism and the complexities of motherhood in songs such as "Pretty Hurts," "***Flawless," and "Blue." This album also includes some of Beyoncé's funniest, and sexiest, adlibs. During the hit "Drunk in Love," she interrupts Jay-Z's rap with the now famous word "surfbort"—a name for a sexual position that sees women literally on top. As with *I Am... Sasha Fierce*, in her self-titled album she explores how all these aspects of womanhood exist in harmony. Just because she has become a mother does not negate her identity as a sexual being, and with this self-titled album, she shows us that she most definitely is just such a being. Women are not one thing, yet in Hollywood monolithic images of women are so prevalent. There is a perception that women are either the virgin or the whore, the career lady or the mom. With this album she beautifully highlights how we are not obligated to give up anything we are to become more, including our sexual identity and pleasure. In telling her story so intricately and personally with this album, she encourages listeners to embrace the entirety of their experience also.

In 2014 Beyoncé graced the cover of *Time* magazine.[10] In a black-and-white image, she wore a white two-piece set with a sheer shirt and looked directly into the camera. Her expression was both carefree yet so intense, and her legs were bare and strong. However, rather than people seeing this cover as a beautiful image of a stunning Black woman, the picture sparked a conversation. The conversation was about how much of Beyoncé's body was hers to show, about this increasingly sexual side of Beyoncé that audiences were witnessing, and whether or not it was "appropriate." Some argued that the magazine should have celebrated her success, not her body, as if the two cannot be celebrated simultaneously, as if the article inside the magazine did not do exactly that.[11] The people who argued that we should be discussing her talent not her body then ironically spent a lot of time discussing her body. Some people were even angry about her facial expression, flawed by her audacity not to smile. Many argued that as one of the most visible Black women of the time she had a responsibility to cover up, to be respectable, and to counter some of the stereotypes that surround us. I would argue none of this is her responsibility. Some of my favorite thinkers have even argued that her overt sexuality is anti-feminist; I argue the opposite. Black women's agency is so often stripped from us, and we are either overly sexualized or completely desexualized. So, Beyoncé owning this aspect of her life as a "grown woman" is completely within her right, and this ownership is empowering and certainly feminist.

What is of huge significance is that Beyoncé has continued to be unapologetically sexual in terms of her lyrics and visual output as she has become a mother and entered her forties. Women in the entertainment industry have spoken about feeling invisible when they leave their twenties. This invisibility can hit them when their body has the audacity to change, when they have a child, or simply when all the laughs that they have been blessed with show up on their face. Actresses who were once the romantic leads become witches, or the mothers of the romantic leads. Meanwhile men are hired to play the leading man opposite actresses twenty years their junior. Singers who were once in short dresses now grace "legend" stages in long gowns and are forced to discuss their legacy while still alive. Importantly, Beyoncé has not compromised anything while going through these life changes in terms of her wardrobe or the subject matter of her songs. I don't want to write about how good she looks for her age—that is irrelevant. The point of my argument is far more important than that. The sexual liberation she exudes in her music and visual output does not have an age limit, and this a feminist statement. She is an example of how to age not just gracefully but authentically. Her sexuality has come with her through all her life stages.

With *Lemonade*, released in 2016, she explores the impact hurt and betrayal can have on someone's sense of self and sexuality. A devastating part of betrayal is the impact it has on your sense of self as a sexual being, and a part of the healing she explores in

Lemonade is getting reacquainted with this aspect of herself. Songs such as "6 Inch" see Beyoncé, or at least the protagonist we follow during *Lemonade*, reengage with her sexuality as part of her journey of healing. *RENAISSANCE* explores sexuality in a completely new way as the entire album is a love letter to the queer community and invites us all to find sexual liberation and freedom within ourselves. "VIRGO'S GROOVE" and "SUMMER RENAISSANCE" reverberate a sense of complete sexual freedom in their overt celebration of Black queerness due to the lyrics and 1970s disco-inspired sound. In *RENAISSANCE*, sexual freedom is not just something she explores in the context of women; she champions a community that has been demonized because of their sexual identity. This album is an argument that sexual freedom is for everyone and inherently political. In *COWBOY CARTER* she explores the complicated history of America as well as her Texan heritage and love of country music, but sexuality also is explored alongside these themes. "DESERT EAGLE" is arguably her most explicit song yet with its graphic description of sex in a car. In a culture that seeks to desexualize or over-sexualize Black women, she refuses to minimize or leave behind her sexuality as her music matures and explores different themes. Even as she explores political movements and musical genres, her sexuality travels with her and is never something she runs from, and why should it be since it's a part of her journey and all our journeys?

Whenever Black women's bodies are being displayed in popular culture, unavoidable and horrific power imbalances are involved. After all, how do we celebrate and move body parts that were once displayed in zoos? This history has kept Black women from ownership of their own bodies, but Beyoncé's lyrics and visuals place her in a position of control over her body *and* sexuality. What's more, both lyrically and visually there is little to no focus on or pandering to the male gaze. Beyoncé frequently sings about her own pleasure and what *she* wants to do, often asking her partner to do nothing but watch. Her videos often show her dancing with only women, far from the video vixens who exist to do nothing but drink champagne on a yacht. Beyoncé is undeniably sexual but not defined by this sexuality, and she embraces all aspects of womanhood. In astrology, the planet of Mars is said to rule both sexuality and anger, which shows that both aspects of the self are so close. It is also telling that the most passionate emotions are the ones Black women are most demonized for expressing. Whatever one may feel about her *Time* cover or the "provocative" dance in the "Crazy in Love" video, in Beyoncé's music I personally find the freedom to embrace passion in all its forms. Does Beyoncé's discography eradicate power imbalances and the way society treats Black female sexuality? No, unfortunately not. After years of conditioning, we will need more than music to shift the stigma around our bodies. However, her work changed how I view mine, and for a piece of art, I think that's quite an impact. One body of work cannot change history or force people to have a more nuanced understanding of Black female sexuality. However, her choreography and skintight leotards have encouraged many of us to care just a little less about how we dance in a club. Ultimately, if popular culture has been a part of the degradation of the Black female body, then it must be a part of its celebration.

Years after her *Time* cover, Beyoncé accompanied her daughter Blue Ivy Carter to a red carpet event for her film debut in *Mufasa*, a *Lion King* prequel. Blue Ivy wore a stunning floor-length ball gown to celebrate the occasion. I and all her internet aunties were proud of this child who has grown up in the public eye making her own artistic endeavors. However, people, predictably, called Blue Ivy's outfit inappropriate and "too grown." Adults argued the child was drawing too much attention to her body while they discussed her body. The shame often leveled at Beyoncé now centered on Blue Ivy, an awful kind of inheritance. While there is a conversation to be had about the images of female celebrities we see and how they are sexualized far too young, there was something so ridiculous in the controversy around this long and formal dress. Even if the outfit was age inappropriate, which it was not, I think we must all agree that the way to counter the over-sexualization of women and girls is not to police them further. I think we must all also agree on the right to bodily autonomy. The answer to countering it is not to force shame upon anyone, whether that is a famous child in a ball gown or a sixteen-year-old girl in a school uniform. These so-called solutions and respectability politics fail for many reasons, mainly because those determined to control our bodies have never considered consent or what we are wearing. Our images will be consumed by people who project old racist ideas onto us, but that is not and cannot be our problem. Whether there are cameras on us or not, our bodies exist to do nothing except what we want them to, and that is one lesson I certainly take from Beyoncé. This lesson is also why I have decided to start here, with the glory of her body and all our bodies—long may they dance.

FEMINIST

In 2014 Beyoncé performed at the MTV Video Music Awards (VMAs). She performed her song "***Flawless" and stood in front of a huge sign that said Feminist. The sign was large and white, and her stance was defiant as she stood with her hands on her hips in front of the neon sign and the voice of Nigerian writer Chimamanda Ngozi Adichie spoke about how we should *all* be feminists. Adichie noted the different ways in which the world tries to shrink girls and what we can all do to mitigate this damage. As I watched this performance it struck me that self-confidence is not something girls are often praised for, a point Adichie makes in her TEDx talk that Beyoncé sampled for the song "***Flawless" and this performance.[1] Adichie's message is that women should be able to focus on themselves, not men or external validation. The talk is a call for girls to live on their own terms, a reminder that they do not exist only to be of service to men and that a woman knowing her worth is a good thing. The talk ends with Adichie imploring everyone to call themselves feminists. She does this by stating the dictionary definition of *feminism*: "a person who believes in the social, political and economic equality of the sexes."[2]

I remember watching Beyoncé during that performance. I remember thinking what a complicated word "feminist" was. At the time, I was part of the feminist society at my university, and I can tell you that the word was not greeted with openness. To call yourself a feminist was, and often still is, met with confrontation and misunderstanding. I would have conversations where I would be asked to define the word, detail the exact type of feminist I was, and dissect what exactly that word meant for me. These are things I still struggle to define now, let alone at nineteen years of age. I'm a confident person, but in my early twenties my politics were evolving to say the least, and trying to make a word fit when other people had such strong ideas of what it meant was a challenge. For these reasons and others, I posted the image of Beyoncé's silhouette in front of that word on my social media. I did this as much for myself as well as the others who may see it. I did not, and still do not, have the intricacies of my understanding of feminism completely clear, but I knew that "feminism" and "womanism" are words to claim proudly and stand in front of.

Gradually more people have begun to claim the label "feminist," and as someone who uses both feminist and womanist to describe myself, I have seen the reception to these terms soften since that day Beyoncé performed. However, with more people claiming the label "feminist," the expectations we place on those who proudly wear this moniker increases also. I do not wish to get into the intricacies of who can or cannot call themselves a feminist or activist, particularly when it comes to celebrities, but I do think the idea that Beyoncé has only claimed this label recently and without authenticity is not valid. For those of us who have been paying attention to Beyoncé's work, to the way she owns her body onstage and is rightfully shameless about doing so, seeing her call herself a feminist was not surprising. Whether she was exploring romantic relationships or feeling great before a night out, these themes of empowerment have been present in Beyoncé's work since she was in Destiny's Child. Songs such as "Independent Women Part 1" prove that feminism has been a part of her career and messaging from the beginning. With her solo anthems like "Run the World

(Girls)" and "Formation," she has continued to celebrate female strength, resilience, and unapologetic self-confidence. "Freakum Dress," "If I Were a Boy," "Upgrade U," "Baby Boy," "Naughty Girl," and "Single Ladies" explore themes of female empowerment and independence—both financial and emotional. Eliana Dockterman wrote for *Time* magazine that "Beyoncé has become the embodiment of modern feminism for a generation that has been reluctant to claim the word."[3] However, I don't think this is something she has recently just "become." Through her lyrics and performances, Beyoncé has uplifted women of all ages, backgrounds, and experiences, inspiring them to embrace their power and stand tall in the face of adversity (in heels if possible).

Recently, the way she explores these themes has developed and grown into songs like "MY POWER" and bodies of work such as *Lemonade* and *RENAISSANCE*. Her feminist messaging has become more personal and grounded in her own journey of motherhood. Whether it's in a ballad that explores the emotional trauma of being cheated on or a chart-topper that instructs women to not settle for less than they deserve, her identity as a Black woman has dominated her discography throughout her entire career. Her songs help women to find their confidence and sexuality, and the independent woman and even warrior-queen motifs remain a staple of her work. As her discography has developed and evolved, becoming more personal and more intricate, these themes of empowerment, specifically for Black women, have only grown more integral to her work. For me it is crucial that she has always used her songs and lyrics to embrace themes of feminism and empowerment in a cultural climate that often shames Black women for doing so. Something in her work has always seemed to give me the permission to be "more," whatever my "more" may be. I shouldn't have needed the validation that came with Beyoncé claiming the feminist label I had been berated for claiming, but as a young university student watching her perform, I felt that moment certainly help me claim feminism and care less about how I may be received for doing so.

To understand the gravity of Beyoncé standing in front of that sign and claiming the title of feminist, we must look back at her early discography. After she sang about expectations from romantic partners and the beauty of independence with Destiny's Child, these themes of female self-sufficiency carried on into her first solo studio album, *Dangerously in Love*. As is clear from the name, the album focuses a lot on love with tracks including "That's How You Like It" and "Crazy in Love" featuring Jay-Z, as well as the title ballad, "Dangerously in Love 2." Aside from being an ambitious, wildly creative yet successful solo album, it also set the tone for her relationship-empowerment anthems that would come to be a staple of her career and a lifeline to many. I would argue this was especially apparent in the song "Me, Myself and I." Among the love ballads on the album, which are still rightfully beloved today, "Me, Myself and I" is a standout track and gives a very different message of independence. When she sings this song live, she opens with an instruction for women to sing along with her. The lyrics and video follow a woman in distress after being cheated on but ultimately finding strength within herself.[4] In an album so focused on love, the song serves as a reminder that we all have worth regardless of romantic love. Even now when she introduces the song on stage, she reminds audiences that the most important relationship we ever have is with ourselves. In a slightly less mature expression of emotion, in the video for the song she keys a man's car while in a floor-length gown. In doing so she holds space for the hurt and betrayal before beginning the journey to self-respect.

With *B'Day*, the themes of empowerment and liberation continued to be a staple of her work. This album also brought us perhaps one of the most iconic Beyoncé songs of all time, "Irreplaceable." The song explores similar themes to "Me, Myself and I" as she sings about being cheated on and finding her own power in the ending of an unhealthy romantic relationship. However, this song represents a more confident and less solemn Beyoncé. There is no crying, no regret, just hair flips and an unflinching belief in herself. The video and the lyrics instruct the cheating partner to remove his things from their home; however, the lyrics also highlight her financial independence. Throughout the song she repeatedly reminds the partner of everything she bought and her ability to find someone else like him. She instructs the partner in question to place everything he owns in a box, specifically a box located "to the left"—which is still an often-used phrase today. In all these songs she encourages women to ask for what they deserve in their romantic relationships.

Also on *B'Day* is the song "Upgrade U." I find this song to be one of her most explicit descriptions of female empowerment in a romantic context. During the song she discusses just how much she brings to a relationship and how much her partner needs her. The song is a testament to how she can turn everything in his life around for the better. Given the context of how devalued women can be in relationships, this song is an antidote. In the song she compares this dynamic to that of the Civil Rights Movement. In one lyric she describes how men may have "led" the movement, but women were guiding it, or keeping the tempo, despite not getting credit for doing so. From a historical perspective, while this is just a lyric in a pop song, its message is true. The work of women activists such Jo Ann Robinson and Ella Baker has long gone unidentified and undervalued in discussions of the Civil Rights Movement. For example, despite Ella Baker's essential contributions to the Student Non-violent Coordinating Committee, her legacy is often overshadowed by men in the movement. History also often neglects to acknowledge the work of Jo Ann Robinson and her bus boycott. Some of Beyoncé's lyrics, such as when she says she will let her man take the lead role and the inclusion of a rap verse by Jay-Z, may seem to counter some of these feminist messages, but it is hilarious and fitting that he is barely even in the video for "Upgrade U" and Beyoncé lip-syncs his verse. Overall "Upgrade U" is a rallying cry to acknowledge the work women do, both in terms of romantic relationships and on a broader societal level.

In *I Am... Sasha Fierce* Beyoncé fully embraces her onstage alter ego, Sasha Fierce, who is not only sexually liberated but the very definition of fierce. One disk of the double-disk album is emotional, featuring the Beyoncé we have come to know and love and blending R & B and mid-tempo pop songs. The other disk is more mainstream and sees her fully embrace the confidence that her alter ego grants her. This duality is even represented through the album artwork. There are two covers: The front one shows a stripped-back Beyoncé with minimal makeup and a more neutral facial expression, while on the back cover we have Sasha Fierce in a leotard with big hair that defies gravity and a dramatic smoky eye. These two images represent what is so good about the album, that it is a love letter to the duality of womanhood. If I was to summarize Beyoncé's feminism, I would describe it as granting women the permission to be the loudest and most confident version of themselves while holding space for the emotions that can often lie under the surface. It is this duality that is so beautifully showcased in this album.

This album is also a love letter to her career and her success—Sasha Fierce is, after all, her stage alter ego—and this confidence in her career is empowering. She has never been defined by anything other than her talent. The music video for "Diva," another iconic song from the album, opens with a two-part definition of the word diva on the screen, the first part reading "a successful and glamorous female performer or personality <a fashion diva>." This definition makes the point that the term "diva" is used as a way to punish women for their success.[5] Similarly, a "diva" in the public lexicon means a difficult woman who thinks too highly of herself and is almost impossible to please. This negativity around so-called divas is what Beyoncé subverts with the song and video. As well as the definition that opens the video, the lyrics see Beyoncé discuss how when men have the same attributes that make women divas, they are called "hustlers." The song makes the point that there is a double standard that exists for women. Beyoncé also uses this song to express the confidence and self-belief that often gets women labeled as divas. She describes how she is on every radio and has been in the industry since the age of fifteen, aligning ambition and success with her womanhood, not in opposition to it. The song is an ode to her career and to all women who express confidence in themselves without shame. Toward the end of the song Beyoncé specifically sends love to ladies that like to "talk back," and as someone often called mouthy, I think it is high time that women who talk back get more love. Beyoncé's brand of confident feminism in *I Am... Sasha Fierce* is defined by duality, agency, and a bold reclamation of femininity as power.

"Single Ladies" is another highlight of this album and embodies these messages, while songs such as "If I Were a Boy" and "Halo" display vulnerability as a part of our strength. With this album Beyoncé said yes, we are fierce, but we are not *just* that. With complexity at the heart of this album, Beyoncé doesn't offer a single definition of feminism. Instead, she asserts that women contain multitudes—softness and steel, heartbreak and defiance—and she gives us the freedom to be all of it.

The artwork to *4*, her album released in 2011, features Beyoncé and her signature fan-swept hair. As all aspects of her work continue to evolve and grow with her discography, the themes of gender and sexism in *4* are similarly developed. The album features a mixture of ballads and pop party songs, including "Schoolin' Life." For me, "Schoolin' Life" stands out on an album that features a lot of ballads about love and loss such as "Rather Die Young" and "Love on Top." "Schoolin' Life" is an upbeat song that is a dedication to women at every part of their journey. With the lyrics Beyoncé speaks specifically to women in their twenties as well as women in their forties. As women are often shamed for aging, especially in the entertainment industry, this song praises the wisdom and experience that aging can bring you rather than viewing it as something to be feared.

Notably, *4* also features the song "Run the World (Girls)." The catchy call-and-response of the song is widely recognized. In the song, Beyoncé highlights the power of women, how we are strong enough to give birth and go back to work, how we are the real nation builders. The music video opens with a visual of the back of Beyoncé's hair as she rides a horse; as Beyoncé is a spiritual person, this image always makes me think of the strength card in a tarot deck.[6] This card usually depicts a woman with a lion and is supposed to give the reader the strength they need on their journey. Later in the video, in what I believe to be a more overt reference to this tarot card, she poses with a lion. To this day I am still unsure if the lion in the video is real. My research tells me that it is in fact not a real lion and was created with special effects. However, I believe the lion to be real and personally will not accept any arguments to the contrary. The setting for the video is an apocalyptic war zone, and while the warrior-queen motif is common in Beyoncé's work, her presence in this video is the epitome of that imagery. She wears a gladiator-themed outfit and a crown, of course, above her bleached eyebrows. In this dusty yet beautiful setting, the video takes the form of a dance battle.

The entire video—including when she sets fire to a car—is an exploration of the endless power she tells us that we as women possess. The enemy in the video is the riot cops, who ultimately fail to contain the power and dance moves of Beyoncé's team of women. In keeping with the rest of her work, the video features intricate and recognizable choreography. As with "Single Ladies," there is no need to focus on clever cuts and over-editing. Beyoncé can dance, so the camera stays on her. The choreography is suitably sharp, fitting the song with hands on hips and chest out and proud. The routine is sexy and strong, with neither of these aspects detracting from the other. The video features the Tofo Tofo Dance Group: a male dance group from Mozambique who Beyoncé discovered on YouTube. The group was flown to Los Angeles to teach Beyoncé and her dancers their native dance moves and appear in the video. Beyoncé won the MTV Video Music Awards Best Choreographed Music Video Award and the Soul Train Music Awards Best Dance Performance Award in

2011 for the video, which would come to be one of many defining moments for her career.

During the 2011 Billboard Music Awards, Beyoncé took to the stage for a performance of "Run the World (Girls)." She begins by loudly telling her audience with her hands on her hips that men have been given the power to rule the world.[7] She stands in front of an image of a lion, but it's just her on stage in a silver minidress with black feathered sleeves, fiercely feminine. Slowly but surely the screen behind her turns into visuals that she interacts with. Drumsticks appear; she uses them. Wings appear, so she flies. I cannot describe or overestimate the level of precision she mastered to interact with these effects as perfectly as she did. In another visual effect, mirror images of her perform the routine next to her. Essentially, she becomes her own backup dancer—her own army. Then she is joined by an army of women and lions. She proclaims, "Ladies, our revolution has begun," and I don't know if the revolution involves very wealthy women on stage with expensive visual effects—but, God, I was tuned in.

When Beyoncé released her self-titled album, it was clear that its explicit and sonically experimental sound and creative collaborators truly elevated her work and the themes of feminine power. The album includes some notable ballads but also songs such as "Drunk in Love" that carry on the theme of her exploring sexual intimacy in a way that prioritizes female pleasure. "Grown Woman," a bonus song originally recorded for release on *Beyoncé*, sees her proudly exclaim that she is a grown woman who has agency and can do whatever she wishes, which is essentially the thesis of the album. However, for me one of the highlights of the album, especially when I do think about themes of feminism in her work, is how it opens with the song "Pretty Hurts." "Pretty Hurts" is more than a good song and brilliant vocal performance by Beyoncé; it's a dramatic exploration of feminine beauty and the double-edged sword it so often offers. Beyoncé discusses these beauty standards through the lens of the beauty pageants that she grew up in.

The video for "Pretty Hurts" opens with women getting ready for a beauty pageant as they unhappily apply makeup and use hairspray on their bathing suits.[8] As Beyoncé enters the stage, she plasters a big smile on her face before being judged by men at least double her age—the point is intentional and clear. As we see this story unfold, the lyrics lament how often what is in your head doesn't matter, as beauty is the most valuable commodity for women. Other lyrics are even more explicit, discussing how magazines like *Vogue* say that thinner bodies are better. The point of the song lies in one of its closing lines—"perfection" is the disease of the nation—and that often it's our souls, not our bodies, that need the "work." During the video Beyoncé expresses that her biggest aspiration in life is to be happy, not pretty or perfect, with this search for self-actualization also present in the rest of the album. The video ends with a clip of a young Beyoncé performing in a beauty pageant. As she thanks the judges and her parents, this footage brings the lyrics as close to home as possible.

"***Flawless," the very song she would perform at the VMAs while declaring herself a feminist, is an upbeat but sultry song that invites women to find their own self-confidence. Importantly, visuals for the song are accompanied by some home footage. Footage of Beyoncé and her girl group Girl's Tyme on *Star Search* opens the song and music video for "***Flawless," as the show's host (an older man with gray hair, large glasses, and a powerful yet nondescript voice) introduces them as "the hip-hop rapping Girl's Tyme."[9] Just as Girl's Tyme are welcomed to the stage and begin their song with "one, two, check," the old footage cuts to Beyoncé in 2014 standing in hot pants and a checked shirt. The lyrics themselves make a statement. During one of the song's refrains, Beyoncé demands that people "bow down, bitches." People have many different perspectives on this lyric (some of which are negative), but I view it as a reclamation of the slur "bitch," an insult to those who continue to underestimate her. "***Flawless" is also a statement that, despite the high-status relationship she's in, she is more than just Jay-Z's little wife, a point she makes many times in the song and album, which is an overt assertion that her recent marriage will not and should not define her. The lyrics to the song represent the kind of anger and defiance that we all sometimes need to harness, all backed up by a typical yet still unique and catchy hip-hop beat.

In addition to Adichie's TEDx Talk, which is sampled in the song, the most iconic and quoted lyrics in it see her assert that she woke up flawless, which also gave us one of the best Instagram captions ever. This line is important because there is so much pressure on Black women to conform to Eurocentric beauty standards that always tell us we are wrong and exclude us, images that a new skin cream should be purchased alongside concealer, relaxer, and other products to make us worthy of being seen and permanently thirty years old. In this context, saying that she woke up flawless is more than just a song lyric; it's a reclamation of a self-confidence that is constantly under attack. As the music video ends, it cuts back to the footage of Girl's Tyme competing on *Star Search*. The host announces that their competitors, the Skeleton Crew, have been awarded a perfect score and have beat Girl's Tyme, who, in the eyes of the judges, did not achieve perfection. It must be said that it is very typical of Beyoncé (a badass) to include footage of her being beaten by some men whose band name is unrecognizable today, while she is now known on a global scale. If ever there was a perfect example of how to not let other people's critiques dim your light or alter your confidence, then it is this music video. Showing an example of her apparently not achieving perfection and coming up against the worst of the industry in a song in which she exclaims that she and all women are flawless is iconic, and quite comical. She invites us all, by way of her past self and current self, to not look for validation externally. She invites us to tell ourselves and everyone around us that we are indeed flawless.

"***Flawless" samples the previously mentioned TEDx Talk from Nigerian writer and activist Chimamanda Ngozi Adichie, the same speech Beyoncé would later play at the VMAs to underscore her performance. In the talk Adichie goes into detail about how girls are taught how to minimize (and apologize for) their accomplishments and intelligence, compared to boys, who are taught that ambition is a virtue. She discusses the division of house labor and the message we send children about traditional gender roles. Adichie also makes the argument that girls are not allowed to be "sexual beings" in the way boys are, and I think this is also a point made in much of Beyoncé's work. Including this section of the talk in "***Flawless" is a very clever and very Beyoncé way to respond to the critique that she is overly sexual. Adichie's talk also supports the lyrics about Beyoncé wishing to not only be defined by her marriage and that girls should be allowed and encouraged to aspire to more than marriage.[10]

Because her ballads often focus on romantic love, some view Beyoncé's music in opposition to feminist progress. There is an argument that Beyoncé's artistry is too defined by men to be called feminist. Adichie herself is on record as saying so. I disagree. If we are to believe the TEDx Talk Beyoncé quoted that we should all be feminists, then it stands to reason that there will be countless types of feminism. However, I completely understand those who do not personally identify with Beyoncé's modern, high-heeled, bejeweled feminism, especially Black women. I also understand those who think celebrity culture and progressive politics are diametrically opposed and should stay this way. But I cannot deny what I do take from her work personally. Ultimately, I am not here to debate whether Beyoncé, or anyone else for that matter, is a feminist. The perception and use of that word is complicated and now comes with a not solely unreasonable responsibility to be aware of all the issues impacting women at all times. I also believe all of us need to find our own definitions for what our activism looks like outside of celebrity culture and the parasocial relationships we are encouraged to build with celebrities. That being said, I cannot and will not deny what countless others and I have taken from her music.

I believe it is easier to see the feminism in her later work, in the visuals of *Lemonade* and the political heart of *COWBOY CARTER*, but feminism has always been at the center of her music. I personally feel at my most free when dancing to a song from *4* or crying to a song from *Lemonade*, and for that I am grateful. Isn't the gift she has given every girl who has taken something from her work feminist? All I can tell you is that I personally have found empowerment in these lyrics, in the way men leave a dance floor when "Single Ladies" starts to play, in the way "Schoolin' Life" reminds me to be proud of every version of who I have been and who I will be. Beyoncé's feminism isn't academic or flawless; it is simply a part of her music as much as anything else in her life. So when Beyoncé stood in front of a sign that said Feminist on a world stage, I loved it, and I wore a T-shirt that said Feminist the day after. Did this action change the world? No, but it felt damn good.

EVEN PEOPLE WHO DON'T LIKE BEYONCÉ LIKE "SINGLE LADIES"

I confess that "Single Ladies" is not one of my favorite Beyoncé songs. I know this opinion is not a controversial one among the Beyhive. However, in the world outside the Hive, where most people don't think about Beyoncé as much as I do, I am aware this song is a major moment in her career as well as in popular culture more generally. I've been to (white) parties where this is the only Beyoncé song I hear all evening—it's a travesty to me, but I am not always permitted rights to the playlist. Cousins with whom I have little in common will drag me to the dance floor when they hear the song's introduction, and for the three minutes and ten seconds of the song our differences will somewhat cease to matter. Sure, if these cousins allowed me, then I would love to discuss the themes of *Lemonade* and ask what they think of her shifting the very definition of what country music is. However, in certain rooms and at certain parties I will take all the Beyoncé I can get—and if that is "Single Ladies," then I will dance to it. Putting aside my love for the *Lemonade* era and the gritty sounds of her self-titled album, the reach and success of "Single Ladies" is undeniable. The beat is catchy, and both the song and video are a masterclass in pop music. The lyrics invite women to find their own worth outside of romantic relationships and to leave relationships that aren't serving them and men who will not commit. This song, as opposed to her others that focus on heartbreak, is about demanding respect and commitment from partners. I would go as far as to argue that the lyrics are somewhat of a rallying cry for the disrespected.

The song is great, but the music video has gone down in history due the iconic and instantly recognizable choreography and black leotards.[1] The video for "Single Ladies" was integral to its success, and you now cannot think of the song without the video or at least the dance routine in it. For a video that starred Beyoncé, two stunning Black female dancers, and not much else, it had such a huge impact. The release of the video also coincided with the growth of YouTube, which added to its impact; simply put, it went viral. This popularity was not surprising because if there is one song that utilizes Beyoncé's talent as a triple threat (dancer, singer, and actress!), it is "Single Ladies." During the video Beyoncé and the two dancers perform an intricate dance routine to the song. While on the surface this is a simple idea for a music video, the intricacy of the choreography and striking visuals make this one of the most iconic music videos of all time. The choreographer, JaQuel Knight, mixed multiple dance influences including ballet and the strong lines of the visionary choreographer Bob Fosse. The result is a dynamic routine that is instantly memorable. The routine was so intricate that the dancers reportedly went through five pairs of heels while performing the moves during rehearsals and recording the video.[2] The routine was also so fast-paced and detailed that Beyoncé is noticeably out of breath at the end of the video; the audio of her catching her breath is even included. However, along with the complicated routine, the team cleverly included some moves that everyone can replicate. While very few can carry off the full routine like the dancers do, most can wave their hand in front of their face on beat. All anybody needs to do is wear a black leotard and put their right hand on their hip and wave their left-hand in front of their face, and the reference is unmistakable. It is this mixture of clear talent and detail combined with simplicity that made the video a success.

The legacy of the video is enduring. Many music videos are viral at the time they are released and create dance routines everyone wants to do, but very few have the staying power of "Single Ladies." The cultural impact of this video cannot be understated, and you would be hard-pressed to find a wedding where that choreography, or a poor drunken imitation of it, is not performed. In fact, the video was so impactful that it created controversy at the VMAs after Taylor Swift was awarded Best Female Video for "You Belong With Me." As a fan of Beyoncé, and Black women in general, I was disappointed at seeing Swift's video championed over Beyoncé's iconic one, which starred Black women and utilized incredibly intricate choreography. More than that, watching the moment felt symbolic of the industry's disrespect to Black women, including, yes, Beyoncé. We at home were not the only ones who disagreed with this result, however. Rapper Kanye West, in a moment that has gone down in popular culture history, took to the stage to interrupt Taylor Swift receiving her award. West uttered the now infamous words of "Imma let you finish, but Beyoncé had one of the greatest music videos of all time," firmly expressing his belief that Beyoncé should have won.[3] When you consider the choreography, skill, and cultural impact of the video, you can see that his argument is not wrong. However, while the industry does, in my opinion, often fail to give Beyoncé the awards she deserves, later in the evening Beyoncé did win Video of the Year for "Single Ladies." However, before she went on stage a producer apparently told her that it would be nice for Taylor Swift to have her moment given back to her. So instead of being able to give her own acceptance speech, Beyoncé graciously (and in my opinion frustratingly), handed the microphone to Swift, who thanked her team and younger brother's high school. While it is correct that Beyoncé *did* have one of the best music videos of all time, it infuriates me that due to the male ego and her not rightfully being awarded both awards, she was denied her moment. This is just one event that made "Single Ladies" a cultural phenomenon.

Because of the artistry and that fateful night, this video has become widely referenced and talked about in popular culture. One example of the impact of the routine can be seen in a sketch on *Saturday Night Live*. The skit includes Justin Timberlake, Andy Samberg, and Bobby Moynihan as they attempt to become her backup dancers for the iconic video. They arrive on set in the signature black leotards and attempt (and fail) to perform the routine.[4] After they are berated by Beyoncé for their awful attempts at the routine, she dismisses them from the set. The *SNL* sketch ends with them exclaiming "music videos are back." And while the rest of the mock video may be a joke, this moniker is entirely true; music videos *are* back.[5] "Single Ladies" was even referenced by President Barack Obama, who also recreated the dance when congratulating a couple on getting engaged.[6] CNN reports discussed this encounter between the president and the newly engaged couple, saying that everyone would recognize that hand movement, and the correspondent was not wrong.

"Single Ladies" also represented a moment of growth and artistic maturity in Beyoncé's career. She is someone that is consistently raising the game of the entire industry as well as herself, and this song and video are examples of that. I have so much love for her early videos and have worn the Destiny's Child–inspired camouflage pants many times, but the slick perfection and skill displayed in "Single Ladies" was unlike anything she had created previously. It is excellence and a masterclass in how to create pop-culture-defining moments. Far from Beyoncé simply being a great pop or R & B artist, I would argue that the release of this song is the moment when she became a powerhouse. Billboard calls this video "arguably the most legendary video, from the 21st century's greatest music video star" with an "enduring legacy."[7] "Single Ladies" brings the commercialized yet radical femininity and the intricacy and perfectionism of her later albums. When I got engaged to my now wife, I did post a picture of my ring alongside the caption, "she liked it." Are you even part of the Beyhive if you don't post your engagement this way? So, "Single Ladies" may not be my favorite song, but I do love the way it brings people together and the fact that it is one of the only songs that connects some of my favorite people to my favorite artist.

AN ODE TO BEYONCÉ AS AN ACTRESS

A friend of mine, a friend who fears the Hive and thus has chosen to remain nameless, tells me that the Hive is delusional about Beyoncé's acting ability. I disagree. Beyoncé's film debut in *Carmen: A Hip Hopera* in 2001 signified from the start that she wasn't interested in traditional routes often taken by singers venturing into acting. This MTV production—a reimagining of Georges Bizet's opera *Carmen*—blended hip-hop with opera and re-centered a classic tragedy by placing a Black woman's experience front and center. Beyoncé also had a brilliant cast alongside her, including the legendary Mos Def. Beyoncé, still in the Destiny's Child era when she starred in *Carmen: A Hip Hopera*, shone with a rawness, magnetism, and acting skill that transcended the film's stylistic experimentation. Her work the following year in *Austin Powers in Goldmember* as Foxxy Cleopatra was a brilliant, clever, and strategic genre pivot. Rather than taking a role with the unnecessary aim of "proving" herself in a straightforward, serious drama (the route many singers turned actors take to earn critical credibility), Beyoncé embraced camp, humor, fun, and Black retro glamor. Her character, Foxxy Cleopatra, an homage to 1970s Blaxploitation heroines like Pam Grier, was not just comic relief—it was a reassertion of Black power and sex appeal in a genre that had often caricatured it. Beyoncé leaned into parody without mocking the legacy of the figures she embodied and the important role they played in American cinema. This role criticizes the stereotypes Black women in film are often confined to but does so while respecting the actresses that took these roles and often turned them into gold (forgive the pun). These films alone prove my point that Beyoncé is an actress, and a great one. That is not to say that I believe she should have won an Oscar for *Obsessed* (although…), but her contributions to film are undervalued and, also, so fun.

The themes in her films often connect to those in her albums. In popular culture in general but on-screen especially, reflections of Black womanhood are rare. Black women on-screen have a long and complicated history, from the mammy stereotype to the jezebel to the white women pretending to be us and beating their breasts on-screen. As I frequently argue, art exists in a context. This context of degradation of Black women on-screen is embedded in the DNA of Hollywood, and Beyoncé's roles do combat these images. If "Single Ladies" gave wider America a moment to celebrate a Black woman, then so do these films. Whether she's reclaiming images that the Blaxploitation genre forced on Black women, or making a film about the Motown record industry, all these roles in some way expand Hollywood's limited representation of Black women.

I was about twelve when *Dreamgirls* was widely released and distributed in early 2007.[1] As a fan of Destiny's Child with a poster featuring one iteration of the group hanging above my bed, I was naturally obsessively following Beyoncé's solo career, including her role in *Dreamgirls*. I was not tech savvy, but my friend had a way of ensuring we could watch whatever we wanted. All that to say I don't know how we managed to watch this film, or even what screen was used to show it, but my friend and I sat on the floor of my very purple bedroom to watch the masterpiece as Beyoncé, Kelly, and Michelle stared at us from my wall. *Dreamgirls* is based on the 1981 Broadway musical by the same name. It is believed that the musical is loosely based on the Supremes and Diana Ross.

It tells the story of three friends who try to "make it" as a singing group in the record industry in the 1960s and 1970s. One reason the film resonated with me was because it was fitting to see Beyoncé explore the dynamics of being in a girl group so similar to Destiny's Child. In the movie, the abuse and manipulation by the men around them lead to most of the emotional high points of the film as we follow the women trying to break free and control their own talent and careers. There are two standout songs from the film for me, and for most people. One is "And I Am Telling You I'm Not Going," sung by Jennifer Hudson. The other is "Listen," performed when Beyoncé's character Deena uses the song to tell her love interest turned manager that he cannot take her voice and her autonomy. "Listen" was not only a stunning moment in the film, but it also appeared on her album *B'Day*.

Even as the film follows three women and their journey, it also focuses on fame and Black womanhood more broadly. Management pushes Deena to the front of the group due to her more marketable voice (and slimmer and lighter appearance). Regardless, the girls have their song stolen by a white band. As well as the film producing one of the first moments Beyoncé was taken seriously as an actress, Jennifer Hudson's performance throughout is celebrated and won her an Oscar for Best Supporting Actress.[2] Spoiler alert: at the end of the film the girls reject the pursuit of white validation. They ultimately reconcile and achieve their "dreams" of becoming professional singers while remaining authentic. As mentioned, I grew up in a white town, and during that time I don't think I realized how much I needed those two hours of seeing these three stunning Black women reject the very notion of assimilation.

These moments are wonderful, but it's the end of the film that is most cemented in my memory. The girls reconcile with Effie White (played by Jennifer Hudson) and invite her back on stage to sing in their farewell performance. Effie gets her long-awaited applause alongside Deena. Even at my young age I recognized that the film was more than glitz, glamour, great music, and escapism; it was real. The dresses, the stunning vocals, the female friendships overcoming obstacles placed by men—it was all so decadently fabulous. To my young mind, I was seeing money, effort, and care being put into a Black film (apparently the production budget was \$70 million[3]). *Dreamgirls* is not just a great film with exceptional performances; it's an exploration of the way fame impacts Black women and the theft of Black creativity, themes Beyoncé would go on to increasingly explore in her music.

David Sims writes for *The Atlantic* that Beyoncé's role as Etta James in the 2008 *Cadillac Records* is her "career best" acting performance.[4] Written and directed by Darnell Martin, *Cadillac Records* is a biographical drama that explores music from the early 1940s to the late 1960s, a very important period for Black musicians. Specifically, audiences follow the life of Leonard Chess, a Chicago-based record-company executive. The film follows him and a small number of the Black musicians who recorded for Chess Records—including Etta James. Beyoncé recorded five songs for the soundtrack, including a cover of Etta James's "At Last," which became the lead single of the soundtrack album. The emotional depth of the role and the personal struggled portrayed allowed Beyoncé to truly shine as an actress *and* singer, resulting in a stellar (and well-reviewed) performance.

In the *Atlantic* article, David Simms argues that Beyoncé has "hardly" acted since, and on that point I do disagree.[5] Beyoncé has acted in many films, such as *The Pink Panther* and *Obsessed*.[6] *Obsessed* is a film released in 2009 and is considered a psychological thriller. It may not be as critically acclaimed as *Dreamgirls* or *Cadillac Records*, but it has a cult following that I consider myself a part of. The general plot is that Idris Elba's character, Derek Charles, is married to his ex-assistant Sharon Charles, played by Beyoncé. It quickly becomes apparent that Derek's new assistant, Lisa Sheridan (Ali Larter), is obsessed with him. This leads to Sharon naturally assuming they are having an affair and telling Derek to leave their home. When he asks Sharon where he should go, she answers, "To hell, but until then I suggest the Four Seasons," before slamming their front door in his face. This is one of the best lines of cinema ever—fight me. Lisa later breaks into their home when Derek is away, and the climax of the film is a physical showdown between the two women.

To be fair, it is important to note that the film did not have great ratings. Some critics argue that Lisa's obsession with Derek seemingly comes out of nowhere. While it is clear she is suffering from poor mental health, the character is without a backstory and is never truly understood. However, one thing critics loved was this final fight. It won an MTV Movie Award for Best Fight. During the fight, which Beyoncé pulls off in fitted jeans and a waistcoat, she states that she will wipe the floor with Lisa's "skinny ass," and I still smile every time I hear the line. This isn't just a funny line that my friends and I often quote; it is a statement about beauty standards and the movie equivalent of "Becky," a name that will be discussed later. It wasn't just us; critics loved the fight scene because it is well choreographed and shot. In a movie that could be described as predictable (though I never described it that way), the fight scene wasn't. Granted, this film may not be as culturally impactful as *Dreamgirls* or as celebrated as Beyoncé's performance as Etta James in *Cadillac Records*, but I do think *Obsessed* is an important film.[7]

So, to answer my dear friend's point—is the Hive delusional about Beyoncé's film career? Perhaps. But from *Dreamgirls* to *Obsessed* and *Pink Panther*, Beyoncé has given Black girls wins on-screen and roles that have shown the complexities of Black womanhood in an industry that consistently seeks to flatten it. From turning the Blaxploitation genre on its head to a nuanced and skilled depiction of Etta James, Beyoncé's acting career has more than earned the right to be taken seriously. It is also undeniable that *Lemonade*, *BLACK IS KING*, and her tour visuals all draw upon this acting career. Beyoncé's acting career should not be viewed as a footnote; it's a frame. And when you look again—with less bias and more attention—you will see that she's been performing with purpose all along.

ACT II

BLACK IN THE SPOTLIGHT—HOW BEYONCÉ REDEFINED BLACK REPRESENTATION IN POPULAR CULTURE

"FORMATION" AND FLOODWATER

In 2016, shortly after Beyoncé performed "Formation" for the first time at the Super Bowl, *Saturday Night Live* joked about Beyoncé "turning" Black and the reactions to her unapologetically Black new music.[1] In a sketch that is, in my opinion, one of the best things *SNL* has ever done, its actors created a mock trailer for a horror movie entitled *The Day Beyoncé Turned Black*. The sketch sees white people react in fear and shock to "Formation," fleeing their homes and wondering what other celebrities might also "secretly" be Black. The sketch shows clips from the video for "Formation" that reference the Black Lives Matter movement as white people scream and claim that they did not know Beyoncé was Black. One white woman in the video asks "What about 'Single Ladies'?" in a fearful voice, as comedic legend Kenan Thompson simply looks at her and states "She was Black in that." Another woman in the mock movie's trailer throws herself against a window in shock, unable to emotionally cope with losing her version of Beyoncé. The Black people in the movie trailer remain unbothered. This sketch works for many reasons. For a start, the reaction to Beyoncé's "Formation" was laughable, especially from places like Fox News, which was expertly parodied by *SNL*. Also, this sketch highlighted how previously Beyoncé had in many ways been everything to all people—the universal face of girl power—and with this music she began to embrace her Blackness in a much more undoubted way.[2]

There are certainly moments where Beyoncé has chosen to address issues of race in America more overtly, such as with her visual albums *Lemonade* and *BLACK IS KING*. At this point in her career (perhaps due to her own security or the political climate) she explores race much more explicitly. While this chapter will mainly discuss songs from these two albums, this is not to say that previous songs are separate from the issue of race or are removed from her experience as an African American woman. As usual, Kenan Thompson is correct: Beyoncé *was* Black in "Single Ladies." While exploring Blackness in Beyoncé's music, it's important to note that she has sung every song as a Black woman. As noted in prior chapters, the empowerment in "Single Ladies" and the joy in "Freakum Dress" is Black. Black entertainers are often tasked with not only doing their jobs but doing so with the expectation of uplifting their communities and constantly performing their race. While many joke about Beyoncé "turning Black," this is ultimately reductive because none of her discography is divorced from her identity. Every song in which she has demanded respect from a cheating partner and told us to listen to the power in our own voice is political. As a Black woman, loving and demanding respect *is* about race.

After teasing audiences with an Instagram post, Beyoncé premiered *Lemonade* on HBO on April 23, 2016.[3] If her self-titled album reinvented the visual album, then *Lemonade* elevated this medium even further. Directed by Melina Matsoukas and including poetry from British Somali poet Warsan Shire, *Lemonade* is not only a visual album but a complete work of art. As the music explores the historical impact of slavery and racism on Black love and the Black family, the visuals tell as much of the story as the lyrics and melodies do. The *Lemonade* film is mainly set on the Madewood Plantation, a Louisiana sugar plantation with an undeniably horrific history. The setting is not only the background for the stunning visuals, but throughout the film the plantation is used as a site of reclaimed joy and empowerment. With this film, Beyoncé takes personal issues and places them in the context of the historical denigration that has caused them. Beyoncé is not the only one reclaiming this space in *Lemonade*; we see young Black actresses as well as stars like Serena Williams featured in the film. Perhaps more significantly we also see the mothers of Black men murdered by police officers. The choice to platform these women brought the Black present, Black past, and Black future to the plantation.

What is also important about *Lemonade* is how personal the album is. Beyoncé is typically a very private person, so her providing what appears to be an insight into her personal life following the rumors of Jay-Z's infidelity was an unexpected move. However, far from simply addressing the rumors themselves, she examines the way Black love has been impacted by America's racial hierarchy more generally and turns the conversation into something infinitely more important. The film and songs follow a woman on the path to reconciliation with her partner and sees her navigate the multitude of emotions she encounters on this journey. While this body of work is largely believed to be semi-autobiographical with its references to her and Jay-Z's previous work throughout, it is also about topics and a history that is so much bigger than any one couple. The lyrics and visuals explore themes of trust, love, and how living in white supremacy can block Black people from healing and experiencing love even among themselves.

It is clear throughout that rather than being a response to the rumor mill, *Lemonade* seeks to show just how political the personal can be. The album is broken into chapters including "Redemption" and "Anger," showing how the full spectrum of human emotions is necessary, even the ones Black women are often demonized for expressing. There is something so beautiful and undeniably transformative about *Lemonade* as a piece of art. Audiences see a side of Beyoncé on this album not often shown in terms of her Blackness and her personal relationships, and in doing so, she shows how linked these two aspects of her life are. As we learn, the personal *is* political, and Beyoncé doing a deep dive into the complexities of the African American experience and heartbreak in the same album is a perfect exploration of this relationship.

In *Lemonade* we also see Beyoncé blending genres seamlessly, something she will do more explicitly with *RENAISSANCE* and *COWBOY CARTER*. Two of the most notable examples of this on the album are "Daddy Lessons" and "Don't Hurt Yourself." With these two songs she uses country and rock music to tell the story of *Lemonade*'s protagonist and in doing so she also reclaims whitewashed genres. The film also beautifully explores the impact of Eurocentric beauty standards on Black women and Black love. *Lemonade* is about what white supremacy has taken from Black women, including Black love, and the impact racism has had on the Black family throughout American history. It is these conversations that make *Lemonade* not only Beyoncé's most personal album to date but also her most political. The album was unapologetically for Black people, Black women especially. It is a testament to our beauty and our anger. Among these messages she pays homage to the Black Lives Matter movement. With the songs and accompanying visuals of *Lemonade* we see Black women navigating the tricky floodwater we find ourselves in all too often, and Beyoncé gives us all so much to take with us when we emerge.

Before the release of the film, the album's first single, "Formation," was released on February 6, 2016. Notably, this was during American Black History Month, and nothing is incidental when it comes to Beyoncé's art. While themes of racial identity are present in many of Beyoncé's albums, never have we seen her be so overt about her Blackness and what it means to her personally as she was in "Formation." The video for "Formation" begins with the voice of New Orleans rapper Messy Mya, who was tragically murdered in 2010. His voice asks "What happened in New Orleans?" as images from a Sundance documentary about Hurricane Katrina are shown. Hurricane Katrina was a devastating and deadly Category 5 Atlantic hurricane that caused 1,833 fatalities and roughly $108 billion in damages in August of 2005.[4] As well as being a devastating natural disaster, Hurricane Katrina has come to be a monumental event for the African American community specifically. This is because Katrina disproportionately devastated predominantly Black neighborhoods in New Orleans, such as the Ninth Ward and St. Bernard's Parish. Evacuation notices were given late, residents had very little reason to trust authority figures even when evacuation orders were put in place, and relief efforts were lackluster. This treatment has led many to see Hurricane Katrina as representative of the pervasive racial hierarchy and segregation still plaguing America. Authorities, including the relief team Federal Emergency Management Agency (FEMA), have long been criticized for their slow response to Katrina. Many have made the argument that the response to and coverage of this traumatic event was fueled by racial prejudice. The then senator Barack Obama stated that there was a "failure of the federal Government to respond with care and rebuild with commitment."[5] Kanye West famously stated on live television that the then president "George W. Bush does not care about Black people," in reference to how little was being done to help survivors under Bush's watch.[6] A report from the inspector general of the Department of Homeland Security states that much of the criticism is valid.[7]

Furthermore, as people desperately searched for food to feed themselves and their newly displaced families after the hurricane, news reports stated that they were simply "looting," tarnishing survivors with the brush of criminality.[8] Beyoncé used visuals of a flooded post-Katrina New Orleans to remind us of these grave injustices and highlight the beauty and resilience of the affected communities. In 2016 the effects of the hurricane had disappeared from news channels and the valuable lessons from this disaster remained unlearned. As "Formation" opens, we are urged by Messy Mya to remember what "happened in New Orleans." If these visuals and song can show us anything, it is that Black people have always been survivors of literal and metaphorical floodwaters.

Another key image from the "Formation" video is that of Beyoncé lying on top of a sinking New Orleans police car as it slowly descends into the floodwater. The relationship between the police and the Black community has been one of abuse and violence for centuries, and the New Orleans Police Department were criticized long before Katrina for disproportionately arresting Black people and those from lower-income communities. It is therefore not hard to see and understand the statement Beyoncé is making with these images. During her earlier career and with albums such as *4*, it is certainly harder to imagine Beyoncé sinking a police car to symbolize the neglect of the African American community. Another key visual in the "Formation" video sees a small Black boy dancing unabashedly in a black hooded sweatshirt in front of police, who are dressed in full riot gear. The contrast between the small child and the police who are prepared for war highlights the disproportionate use of force against the Black community, often children. The boy stops dancing and puts his hands in the air, an action followed by the police mimicking his movement of surrender. In case the message was unclear, a clip of graffiti on a nearby wall reveals the message "stop shooting us."[9] These images, combined with Beyoncé's stern facial expression as she lies on top of the sinking police car, speak to the necessity of Black anger and protest. The message is further heightened by the inclusion of the mothers of several young Black men killed by police officers. Sybrina Fulton, mother of Trayvon Martin; Gwen Carr, mother of Eric Garner; Lezley McSpadden, mother of Michael Brown; and Reverend Wanda Johnson, mother of Oscar Grant—a group known collectively as the Mothers of the Movement—are featured in *Lemonade*. Rap and other genres have a long and proud history of shining a light on various injustices and police brutality, but this is less common in the more commercial world of pop. For so long Beyoncé existed in a world where she was all things to all people, like so many pop stars. White audiences had skewed their perception of her to fit their own agenda without challenging it. To them, she was the uncontroversial and beautiful face of girl power with music that provided dopamine and a good time. *Lemonade*, and "Formation" specifically, broke this façade by showing that she cannot be separated from the community she is a part of, and she does not want to be.

As well as shining a light on these injustices, another theme present throughout the entirety of the "Formation" visuals is that of Black self-love. To love yourself fully as a Black woman is a political act, one that requires at times an almost superhuman level of strength and resilience. One arena in which these harsh realities continue to present themselves is in hair. Eurocentric ideas favoring straight or long hair have been present since the time of slavery, with only recently the CROWN Act being put in place to protect against discrimination based on hair. Children are unfortunately not exempt from these Eurocentric beauty standards. When Beyoncé's daughter Blue Ivy was two years old, a petition was created calling for Beyoncé and her husband to "tame" her hair. The argument was that Blue Ivy's hair was "unkempt" and "un neat"—and that her parents needed to maintain it—ridiculous criticism that would rarely if ever be given to a white child. The petition also stated that Blue Ivy's hair was "dry" and "matted." It was not. The child's hair was simply free.[10] Beyoncé chose not to respond online, but instead she sung loudly in "Formation" about how much she loves her child's natural hair, complete with her baby hair and Afros. In the video, this lyric is accompanied by an image of Blue Ivy smiling confidently into the camera with her hands placed defiantly on her hips. Later we see Black children running and laughing, carefree and unconditionally beautiful. This freedom, this carefree joy that so many are lucky enough to associate with childhood, is not often afforded to Black children. Given this context, showing this unconfined Black joy on the faces of these children is arguably one of the most political moments of the video. Another image from the "Formation" video that is forever etched in my memory is that of a group of Black female dancers taking up the entirety of an empty swimming pool with their Afros as large as possible as they lean on each other. It is notable that Beyoncé, who often wears a blonde wig for performances and music videos, instead wears braids for the video. For Black women, hair is not just hair, and the visuals as well as lyrics are a great reminder of why.

Like the whole album, "Formation" is also personal and speaks to the beauty of Black romantic love. In a witty lyric that has come to be typical of her latest work, Beyoncé cheekily sings about rewarding her husband when he pleases her sexually and how she loves his African features including his nose. While lyrics like this may seem misplaced next to visuals of Katrina and police violence, the message of *Lemonade* and certainly "Formation" is that for Black women, love is political and impacted by the context of the historical violence against us. Among anthems such as "Freedom" and "Formation," there are also deeply personal songs and moments during the "Forgiveness" chapter of the album. She talks about removing her wedding ring from her finger and the deep cost of betrayal in a marriage on an album that also speaks about the historic violence the Black community has faced. Black love, both romantic and personal, cannot be separated from what seeks to destroy it.

As well as being an overtly political song, "Formation" is also a fun song. Much of this joy comes from the fact that bounce music is at the heart of it. Bounce music is a genre of music that originated in New Orleans and is often described as a faster-pace style of hip-hop.[11] To honor the power of bounce music and its history, New Orleans iconic queer bounce musician Big Freedia appears on the interludes in "Formation." Big Freedia has been credited with helping popularize the bounce genre, which had largely existed in underground settings since its emergence in the 1990s. She confidently exclaims, over an immediately infectious beat, that she is back, bitch. Later she states that she came to slay, bitch—and that she likes soul food including cornbread and collard greens, bitch. With these fun lyrics and references to classic

Black Southern cuisine, Big Freedia's impact on the song is undeniable (which is no easy feat when you are featured on a Beyoncé song). However, Beyoncé does not let Big Freedia have all the fun. Beyoncé half sings, half raps about twirling on her haters and how they are corny with the many conspiracy theories they create about her and her family, including that they are members of the Illuminati. When thinking about "Formation," it is easy to only consider the images of Katrina and sinking police cars, and while these are significant, so is the Black joy and confidence that Big Freedia and Beyoncé inject into every lyric of the song.

The chorus of the song sees her sing that she slays, all day, following Big Freedia's assertion that she came to slay. Slay is a word that gained popularity among the Black queer community in 1970s and 1980s New York during the height of ballroom culture. The word is typically used to mean to dominate or excel at something, often relating to a performance or outfit.[12] However, this phrase has also now become widely used outside of this community, in part due to the commercial success of drag and ball culture in popular mainstream culture such as the reality TV show *RuPaul's Drag Race*. Despite the role of African American culture in shaping language, when words become popularized credit is not often given to the Black people who shaped the language. These terms can also often be used out of context on social media and by people unfamiliar with the true origins of the terms. Beyoncé invited Black queer icon Big Freedia on the song to use this phrase before also reclaiming it herself. The use of this significant yet overused word further highlights the fact that language is political and another example of the colonization of Black creativity, much like the genres Beyoncé also reclaims on *Lemonade*.

We also cannot discuss the "Formation" visuals without mentioning the Super Bowl performance that took place the day after the song was released. In a performance where she was not *technically* the headline act, Beyoncé took to the stage with her team of Black female dancers to perform the new song. To make the message of the song abundantly clear, her backup dancers were dressed in outfits that paid homage to the Black Panther Party, wearing Afros, berets, and black leather.[13] As the performance begins, they make an *X* formation, an unsubtle reference to Black nationalist and civil rights leader Malcolm X, who is referenced many times in *Lemonade*. Both Malcolm X and the Black Panther Party have historically been denigrated, misremembered, and misrepresented due to their radical championing of Black people. Beyoncé's use of such a large platform to so clearly pay respect to the Black Panther Party and Malcolm X is undeniably political. The perception of Malcolm X as a violent man and the Black Panther Party as a dangerous group persists to this day. Much of Beyoncé's recent work is about reclaiming what has been taken from the Black community, championing these controversial figures, and highlighting the beauty of Black radicalism. What better place to reference an American hero than at the great American game?

However, this performance made a lot of people upset. The former mayor of New York Rudy Giuliani insisted that the performance was insulting to police officers and that Beyoncé should instead have used the platform to build respect for police officers.[14] His comment came despite the fact that nowhere in the performance did she directly mention law enforcement or any of the young people who have lost their lives at the hands of police officers. But ultimately this reaction was not surprising. We find different ways of telling them to stop killing us, and they find different ways to do it and get angry about our response to injustice rather than about the injustice itself. For these reasons, "Formation" is my favorite Beyoncé song—mainly because I adore seeing Black women embrace the full spectrum of human emotion, including anger. The image of Beyoncé's head leaning out the window of a car with braids so long they nearly hit the ground in the video, and her Black Panther–inspired performance of the song was unexpected, yet the excellence of it all was exactly what we have come to expect of Bey.

However, while it may be considered the album's defining song, "Formation" does not open *Lemonade*. Rather, *Lemonade* opens soft with a section entitled "Denial," which includes "Pray You Catch Me" and "Hold Up." "Denial" may be soft, but it is not passive here; it's Beyoncé's clenched resistance to fully acknowledge her pain because doing so would require destroying and leaving behind the version of herself she'd built to survive it. This section marks the threshold between her silence and fury, signaling the beginning of her reclamation of voice and agency that will happen later in the story told in *Lemonade*. These songs and the accompanying poetry see Beyoncé, or the protagonist of the film released with it, in denial about the fact her partner has cheated. In "Hold Up," she wields a baseball bat named hot sauce in an off-the-shoulder yellow Cavalli gown as she strolls down a street and loudly proclaims that she will not let her partner go. All of this occurs while she is channeling the Yoruba goddess Oshun. Oshun is a prominent Orisha (God or spirit in the traditional Yoruba religion) associated with love, fertility, beauty, and freshwater. As Beyoncé channels Oshun in that iconic yellow dress, we see her literally begin a flood, and the theme of water carries on throughout the entire *Lemonade* film.

We then enter the "Anger" chapter of the album. The third song of the album that opens the floodgates to this anger is "Don't Hurt Yourself" and features contemporary rock icon Jack White. At the opening of the song, we hear a commanding drum and bass. The very core of the song, as well as the lyrics themselves, are beautifully aggressive. In the story told in *Lemonade*, this is the part where the protagonist fully embraces her hurt and promises to return it. Beyoncé fully and unapologetically embraces her anger with lyrics claiming that her partner hurting her will only hurt her partner in the long run. She swears and she growls, reclaiming her voice and agency, no longer begging or in denial. Importantly, the song is a rock song, made even more obvious with the inclusion of Jack White and her vocal growling. The rock genre not only fits in with the theme of the song and the protagonist's journey, but it is also a political statement (like *Lemonade* more broadly). The choice of using the rock genre is important as Black people, and women specifically, pioneered rock and roll. However, despite their crucial role in the conception of the genre, Black women are largely ignored and removed from its legacy.

One cannot, or rather should not, discuss rock and roll without discussing the godmother of rock and roll, Sister Rosetta Tharpe. Her pioneering use of distortion on the electric guitar influenced Eric Clapton and Jimi Hendrix, and her vocals influenced Aretha Franklin and Tina Turner. She broke genres, starting in the world of gospel but not being defined by it. During her lifetime she broke records across the American South and across the Atlantic. She played the guitar like "no one else."[15] However, despite this talent and legacy she was placed in an unmarked grave when she died. Furthermore, as of yet, there has been no big-budget biopic about her extraordinary life, and there exists only one biography on her.[16] Also, Tharpe was only inducted into the Rock & Roll Hall of Fame in 2018, forty-five years after her death in 1973, and was not part of its inaugural class of inductees. The erasure of this visionary performer is symbolic of the way Black women's contribution to music has gone unnoticed. Rock and roll *is* a Black genre of music, and Beyoncé's performing a rock song is her reclamation of a genre that has been whitewashed. The decision to reclaim a genre that has been stolen from Black women fits perfectly on an album about the historic denigration of Black women. Beyoncé performing a rock song on this deeply personal and Black album highlights how the US racial hierarchy has stolen not only Black love, but also Black art.

As "Don't Hurt Yourself" continues with its commanding drum and bass, the lyrics see Beyoncé instruct listeners to call her Malcolm X, fully embracing her own power and anger. The visuals take this comparison even further with the inclusion of Malcolm X's voice delivering his famous "Who Taught You to Hate Yourself?" speech in 1962.[17] In this defining speech, Malcolm X asks Black women to consider who taught them to hate themselves and implores them to blame and fight against white supremacy. He states: "The most disrespected person in America is the Black woman. The most unprotected person in America is the Black woman. The most neglected person in America is the Black woman."[18] These lines are quoted in the video, a nod to the theme of self-love and self-protection for Black women in *Lemonade*. In this song in particular, the protagonist fully claims her own power and repeats that she is not average. She concludes that in hurting her, the cheating partner is only hurting himself. She asserts that she is, and will continue to be, fine on her own. While the protagonist at this point in the video is fully embracing her anger, she is still so much more than that one emotion. In many ways these lyrics continue the theme of the quoted speech, and she spends almost the entire song exploring her own attributes and what makes her powerful, referring to herself as both a dragon and a lion. To echo the theme of Malcolm X's speech, the protagonist is not listening to whoever told her to hate herself.

In popular memory Malcolm X is seemingly defined by his anger, but this is a reductive take on his legacy and teachings, which are in fact about hope and unity. Malcolm X was a crucial figure who spoke very eloquently on issues impacting Black Americans, and by including part of his speech from 1962, Beyoncé argues that the historical mistreatment of Black women remains active today. In the song, the protagonist constantly asks her partner who he thinks she is, but by the end of the song it's clear that his view is irrelevant. As the speech from Malcolm X and the lyrics show, the only opinion of herself that matters is her own.

Beyoncé's journey transitions to the "Apathy" section of the album, which includes the song "Sorry." Before looking at the song in its entirety, it is important to note that it opens with a sample from *Swan Lake*, gently playing as we hear more poetry by Warsan Shire. Notably, *Swan Lake* is a ballet about a woman who is cursed to be a swan by day until the curse is broken when she finds true love. The protagonist is tasked with not only saving herself but other cursed women—like the protagonist of *Lemonade*. Both are stories about women being denigrated and eventually cured and healed by love and devotion. The opening visuals of "Sorry" sees Black women with Yoruba face paintings dancing on a bus. Nigerian visual artist and human rights attorney Laolu Senbanjo painted these geometric motifs that have come to be one of the most iconic images of the *Lemonade* film. The choice of a bus as the setting points to the role buses and public transport played in the Civil Rights Movement. It is no accident that a bus is the setting of one of the most defiant and impactful displays of the power of Black womanhood in "Sorry," when Rosa Parks refused to leave her bus seat in 1955 and Claudette Colvin refused to do so earlier that year. Buses were also used by young radical activists during the Freedom Rides in the early 1960s. Buses were certainly settings of defiance but also violence, just like the plantation where many of the other *Lemonade* visuals are set. The shot of Black women dominating this space unapologetically with their Yoruba-inspired face paintings references modern history but also the history that was stolen from enslaved Africans.

The poetry featured in this section of the album has given us some of the most defining moments of *Lemonade*, with Shire asking her partner what he will say at her funeral now that he is responsible for her death. The visuals transition to Serena Williams walking down the stairs of the Madewood Plantation House in a black outfit with long flowing hair. She immediately starts to dance, crouching to the ground and twerking as Beyoncé starts the vocals. She looks straight into the camera, as self-assured as the lyrics themselves. Aside from being one of the greatest athletes of all time who happens to be a Black woman, Serena's role in this video goes deeper than surface-level representation. Throughout her career Serena has been subjected to abuse about everything from her body to her standing up for herself on a tennis court. She is often described using racist animalistic imagery and subjected to the "angry Black women" trope for asserting herself on court. In her own words she states, "I was scrutinized because I was confident, I was Black and I was confident."[19] Serena's public scrutiny is an example of how Black women are not allowed to be excellent in peace, something we have also seen in Beyoncé's career. The visual of Serena, whose appearance, personality, and talent are all often critiqued in the media, dancing during a song about the disrespect Black women face is in many ways the thesis of *Lemonade.*

Beyoncé and Serena are two women who have excelled in their career and refuse to apologize for this. Serena, like the women on the bus, uses dance to reclaim a place of historic brutality by twerking in the parlor room of the Madewood Plantation House, a place of impossible survival. She twerks next to Beyoncé, who sits on a throne, and both women make themselves completely at home. Again, everything is intentional, and twerking specifically has links to their African heritage. For the blog *Progressive Pupil*, writer Ebony Wilkins describes beautifully the West African origins of twerking, specifically from a dance called Mapouka in Côte d'Ivoire. Wilkins also describes how the dance form became popularized in the early 1990s' New Orleans bounce scene that Beyoncé honored with *RENAISSANCE.* Twerking is not just a dance; it is an example of diasporic inheritance and Black feminine expression. Despite the importance of this dance, it is often over-sexualized and misunderstood, and this is why Beyoncé reclaims twerking.[20] During this video, there is not a man in sight; the women are dancing only for themselves while highlighting a body part that Black women have been simultaneously defined by and shamed for. In this instance, dancing is an act of resistance and empowerment. Due to the history of the dance and the very setting of the video, these images are so much more significant than simply Serena Williams twerking in a Beyoncé video. Here, the dance is everything.

The hook of the song is a call-and-response Beyoncé makes to herself where she refuses to apologize or blame herself for her partner's infidelity. She also uses the N-word in the song, which is relatively a new development in Beyoncé's discography and in keeping with the grittier sound and racial themes of *Lemonade*. Her use of the N-word is another way in which Beyoncé has shifted how she engaged with her Blackness during *Lemonade*. She then encourages the other women around her to leave their own romantic partners and instructs them to place their middle finger in their man's face, swearing at him. This can be seen as a development from Beyoncé's previous instruction to wave their bare ring finger in their partner's face in "Single Ladies" to display that they would like the commitment of an engagement ring. Whereas her previous instructions centered on women using their hands to get their partner to commit, now she suggests swearing at them. This play on lyrics from "Single Ladies" is the clearest reference in *Lemonade* to her past discography. Like this reference, previous music from both Beyoncé and Jay-Z is referenced throughout *Lemonade*, further contributing to the semi-autobiographical feel of the album. In the plot of *Swan Lake*, the protagonist must free her community of women, and in *Lemonade* Beyoncé tells women their power and freedom are not found in a partner.

"Sorry" also critiques white beauty standards, a theme that is present throughout the album. After spending the song refusing to apologize for who she is, Beyoncé states that her partner better call a woman she refers to as "Becky" and who is said to have "good hair." Kamryn Z. Bess writes for *Folklife Magazine* that "good hair" has been used to mean "straight" or "looser hair" since at least the 1900s due to its proximity to whiteness and a higher socioeconomic status. While many in the Black community have fought against such norms, Eurocentric beauty standards harm non-white communities, stealing away other cultures and capital and spawning versions of the self-hate that Beyoncé explores in *Lemonade*.[21] "Good hair" in this case references the pressure Black women often feel to change their natural hair to conform to white beauty standards. Throughout the visual album of *Lemonade*, a variety of beautiful Black hairstyles are shown. These images of Black women made the lyric about "good hair" and beauty standards even more impactful. While

"Sorry" certainly catapulted the use of the word "Becky" in the public lexicon, this song was not the first use of that name in music. In Sir Mix-a-Lot's "Baby Got Back," two women—one called Becky—talk disparagingly about a Black woman with a big "butt." A lyric that implores Becky to look at the woman's butt is often referenced and very catchy. Notably the song "Baby Got Back," while hardly a feminist anthem, does champion a body type outside of conventional white beauty standards. Both "Baby Got Back" and "Sorry" use the name Becky to represent how white women are widely considered the standard of beauty. However, while Becky is referenced throughout "Sorry," ultimately, she is irrelevant. Beyoncé tells her partner to call Becky, not as a perceived upgrade, but because he is not worthy of her time anymore. It is this messaging that makes this one of my favorite moments in *Lemonade.* "Sorry" is a song that is the definition of unapologetic as Beyoncé puts herself so far above the forces that seek to bring her down, including white supremacy and the proverbial "Beckys" and the men who chase them.

When thinking about themes of Black Power in Beyoncé's discography, "Freedom" is the all-encompassing song. In the visuals we see Beyoncé begin the song a cappella in front of a small audience of Black women. The rest of the video is also set on the plantation. When Beyoncé utters the word "freedom," the beat drops and the song truly starts. The late Sierra Leonean ballet dancer Michaela DePrince—who made history as the youngest principal dancer at the Dance Theatre of Harlem—takes the stage. The talent of DePrince in her video spotlighted Black women dominating a historically white dance form. The beautiful vulnerability of DePrince dancing combined with images of Black women dining at the plantation demonstrates how vulnerability absolutely has a place next to displays of power and anger, which is in my opinion another central message of *Lemonade.*

The visuals then focus on other Black women, some famous and some not, defiantly posing next to or on top of trees, which play a tragic part of African American history. As Rachel Barns writes for NBC, "elegant oak trees with their hanging Spanish moss may look picture-perfect to a Caucasian, but to someone with African, Native or Latina roots, it may conjure ancestors hanging."[22] Given that the trees in "Freedom" are located on the plantation and were likely the site of such lynchings and terror, this is perhaps the strongest example of reclaiming a brutal history in the entire *Lemonade* film. In the lyrics for "Freedom," the protagonist is in control of everything, including her own tears. Using this control, Beyoncé commands her tears to burst into flames—something hotter and more destructive than sadness. She sings about her determination to wade through waters and ride through borders, calling herself bulletproof. She asks where freedom is and demands that she needs it, before concluding that she can break the chains that bind her by herself.

The song then moves into a verse by Kendrick Lamar. Kendrick Lamar is one of the greatest artists of our generation (and especially of the summer of 2024) whose well-crafted lyrics were awarded a Pulitzer Prize for Music. While he is one of the most talented (and decorated) rappers of the twenty-first century, he has also made it his artistic mission to bring attention to the issues impacting Black people. His song "Alright" is often referred to as the soundtrack to the Black Lives Matter movement because of what it means to the Black community and the fact that it is often sung and quoted at protests. His work is intricately crafted, and he is a master storyteller. Lamar's presence on "Freedom" further signifies that the Black community are central to the story being told in *Lemonade*. In "Freedom," Lamar intricately explores how he and fellow Black men are victimized by institutional racism, and he calls for an end of this structural oppression. He examines media portrayals of Black men and how they are consistently misrepresented by everyone from newscasters to the police. He reaches the conclusion that Black men can reach for perfection and give their all to the world around them, but until freedom is truly acquired, they will still be perceived as a threat.

The duo performed the song at the BET Awards in 2016.[23] The performance opens with Beyoncé's dancers, all Black women, marching to the stage as the voice of Martin Luther King blares. King's voice states, "We refuse to believe the bank of justice is bankrupt. [. . .] So we've come to cash this check." The quote is from a section of his "I Have a Dream" speech not often quoted.[24] It does not tie in so neatly to the perception of King that is often perpetuated and is, simply put, less palatable to white people. It is notable also that it focuses on action rather than dreams. The sound of the BET audience cheering can be heard during this speech as we see the dancers and Beyoncé take to the stage. As the performance starts it is revealed that there is water on stage, water that Beyoncé and her dancers are completely in control of, as in the *Lemonade* film. As Lamar emerges on stage, he begins by reciting lyrics not included in the original song. He raps about forty acres in reference to the famous broken promise made to freed slaves that they would be given forty acres of land and a mule. The entire performance is not a polite request; it is a demand. He finishes his segment by literally and metaphorically kicking the microphone over as Beyoncé, the symbol of Black pop, stands triumphantly behind him. Both the video, as part of the *Lemonade* film, and every performance I have seen of "Freedom" are some of her most powerful performances, and I do not use that distinction lightly. The images of Beyoncé with her long braids hanging out of the back of a speeding car and stomping on water next to Kendrick Lamar are so stunning and encapsulate this era of her artistry.

In the *Lemonade* film, at the end of "Freedom" we hear Jay-Z's beloved grandmother speak about how she has made lemonade from the proverbial lemons that life has given her. The audio clip is a recording from her ninetieth birthday, and I often think about how the clip could have been used anywhere in the film and yet makes so much sense here at the end of this song. Her soft voice takes us from a place of action and righteous anger to a place of celebration, a line *Lemonade* walks seamlessly.

After this audio clip, "Freedom" ends and is followed by "All Night," one of the more romantic songs on the album that explores how Beyoncé (or the protagonist) can trust her partner again after the long journey she's made throughout the album to a loving and satisfying conclusion.

It is reductive and narrow to claim *Lemonade* is the only body of work in which Beyoncé's art discusses race and her experience as an African American woman. It is also important to note that Black artists and other artists of color should not be tasked with discussing race while white artists are not. No one is asking white artists to be a voice for their entire race or to use their art to highlight the beauty of white women. To this extent it annoys me that Beyoncé's work must carry this message. However, in her recent discography Beyoncé has begun to tackle race loudly, and most of the songs on *Lemonade* speak to the necessity of Black anger and Black self-love and joy. While it was not necessary, and she has received criticism from thinkers on all sides of the political spectrum for doing so, for me there has been something very validating in seeing her explore race through her music. What I find most empowering is the exploration of Black female anger because anger is such a demonized emotion for Black women. Not only does *Lemonade* show that this anger is valid and historical, but it also shows that there is so much beauty in it. And in the slow moments in our lives, she encourages us to make sandcastles and immerse ourselves in soft Black love.

It is difficult for me to choose a second favorite Beyoncé album, but it's easy to choose a first: *Lemonade.* The album only continues to grow in my estimations, for the songs I have mentioned here and for all the gorgeous visual and sonic moments in between, for the lemons and the lemonade. While there are many albums of Beyoncé's that I personally believe should have been awarded Album of the Year at the Grammys, the fact *Lemonade* did not receive this award still angers me to this day. It is one of the best explorations of everything that makes us human and what exists as a threat to that very humanity. The album ends with the lead single, "Formation." That is to say that the album ends with a call to action. With this song, Beyoncé invites Black female listeners to take the personal journey of *Lemonade* and use it to step into the beauty of our Black womanhood. Simply put, she wants us to get in formation. During the outro to the video for "Formation," a voice states, "golly, oh lord, look at that water," as the police car Beyoncé has been sitting on finally sinks into the floodwater and Beyoncé once again faces the camera.[25]

Some may believe there is a tension between the playful lyrics and the heavy images on-screen, but I argue that they work harmoniously. The visuals for "Formation" and *Lemonade* are necessarily political. But what the album demonstrates is that the Black experience is not only pain and injustice: it is love and good food and children dancing. If we can take anything away from the *Lemonade* visuals, it is that Black joy, Black love, and Black liberation do not exist in vacuum. For there to be Black laughter there must first be Black liberation, and for there to be Black love there must first be freedom. To love and dance, this community has had to swim through floodwaters, and these images from *Lemonade* remind us of just how deep these waters have been. This is why I can remember exactly where I was when I first saw "Formation," on my friend's bedroom floor, laughing and crying simultaneously, while comprehending the beauty of both.

BEYCHELLA—THE UNIVERSITY OF BEYONCÉ

A new era of Beyoncé began in April 2018 when she became the first Black woman to headline Coachella. Not only was this an incredible show to attend in person (I assume, I wasn't there—ticket prices), but it also gathered an amazing number of viewers at home. The performance is reported to have had 458,000 simultaneous viewers from 232 countries with 43.1 million views in total as well as garnering an incredible response online.[1] I was at home trying to watch the performance on one screen and follow the social media commentary on another. Every tweet on my timeline was about Beyoncé and the pop event of the year, and as I rewatched and delved into not only the performance but the responses to it, I saw why this show had such an impact. As Beyoncé opened the show standing confidently in an outfit inspired by Egyptian Queen Nefertiti, it was clear the show was about to be something special and unique, but very few could have predicted the level of talent on display and the rich history she would bring on stage with her.[2] The show used gospel and soul influences and shone a light on HBCUs (historically Black colleges and universities). A spectacle that resonated so far beyond music, her performance at Coachella was a statement about belonging and identity and the strength found in communal joy and celebration.

A year after headlining Coachella, Beyoncé released the live album of the performance and a subsequent film documenting the process and performance entitled *Homecoming: A Film by Beyoncé* in April 2019.[3] The documentary offered rare personal details about her creative process, even going as far as to share that she was scheduled to headline Coachella in 2017, but she postponed her hosting as she was pregnant with her twins, Rumi and Sir. Her performance in 2018 was a phenomenal production that required over four months of rehearsals for two hours of stage time. The film opens with a quote from esteemed African American novelist Toni Morrison, before moving on to Beyoncé talking about her love for Black colleges and the creative and talented students that attend them. Speaking of her childhood, Beyoncé remarks that it was her dream to attend an HBCU, but her early career was her education instead. Her Coachella performance also celebrated marching bands, which play an important role at HBCUs, as audiences were treated to the sounds of Drumline Live, a Grammy-award-winning HBCU-inspired marching band. During the performance, Beyoncé wore a now iconic sweatshirt with letters from the Greek alphabet in tribute to the Divine Nine. The Divine Nine are the nine historically Black Greek-letter organizations (fraternities and sororities) that make up the National Pan-Hellenic Council. Many of the Black fraternities and sororities were founded at the beginning of the twentieth century at HBCUs and are still thriving today.[4] For this once-in-a-lifetime performance, Beyoncé created her own Black college. Every detail of this college wardrobe was personalized, from that of the band to the dancers to the background vocalists on stage dripping with custom Balmain outfits that were designed to look like college merchandise featuring her initials, BK.

To understand why Beyoncé chose to do this and why it is so significant, one must understand that HBCUs have a long and rich history in America. America's first Black college, the African Institute, was opened in Philadelphia in 1837 by a Quaker philanthropist. It was later renamed Cheyney University and had a specific mission to train teachers and prepare workers for trades. It was one of the first safe spaces for learning in an unsafe country. After the American Civil War more colleges for the formerly enslaved and their children began to open, especially in the Southern states, including the now world-famous Howard University that opened in 1867. These colleges were often sustained by grants and freedmen's societies, as well as churches and benefactors that still contribute today.[5] Throughout America's terrible and long history with racial segregation, these institutions provided education (and so much more) for the Black students when other institutions would not. Today they continue to offer safe spaces for Black students to learn in an environment where they are not minorities and where they are continuously prioritized. These are successful and rigorous academic institutions that continue to attract the best and brightest students who are in search of a world-class education, as well as community. This reputation has led many to refer to Howard as "the Black Harvard" or "the Mecca."[6]

Scholar SeKai Parker spoke to the *New York Times* about how she was offered a place at the prestigious Ivy League Yale University but chose instead to attend Spelman College, a Black Women's college.[7] Her story is not unique as more and more Black students are opting to attend HBCUs regardless of their other options. Parker stated that "learning about my people, from my people, with my people, is such a powerful experience." She speaks of the beauty of having a space centered entirely on her community, even describing how the water in the swimming pool is formulated to be gentler on Afro-textured hair. Over their history, HBCUs have educated most of the nation's Black judges, half of its Black doctors, and 40 percent of the Black members of Congress, as well as former Vice President Kamala Harris. What's more, HBCUs still serve students from low-income backgrounds and pride themselves on their history. Very few people describe the beauty of being at an HBCU better than Howard alum, journalist, author, and activist Ta-Nehisi Coates. In his debut memoir dedicated to his son, he not only calls Howard University his mecca, but he states that walking around the grounds is like hearing multiple versions of "Redemption Song" by Bob Marley sung simultaneously.[8]

Utilizing the vastness of the Coachella stage, Beyoncé included the practice of stepping into her dance routines. Stepping arguably originated from enslaved African communities who used their bodies to create music in the absence of drums and other resources. Simply put, they made the rhythm with their body. According to Richard Smith, one of the founders of the East Coast Step Show in Fayetteville, modern stepping has been practiced since the early 1900s. He states, "Over the years, the styles have changed," before going on to argue that "what makes stepping so significant is it's a particular talent, it's a particular art, particular choreography that is very different from just regular dance or any other type of art that only certain individuals can do. Everybody can't step. It's very difficult to learn and you just got to be very gifted in my opinion."[9] It has also become a way for organizations to show pride and unity in their group and was even featured in Black situation comedies like *A Different World* and *The Fresh Prince of Bel-Air*. The Divine Nine also used song and dance as a call-and-response to uplift audiences. Talking about the inclusion of stepping in the show, Beyoncé stated that "I wanted a Black orchestra, I wanted the steppers" before asserting that "the amount of swag is limitless."[10]

Not only were her theme and choice of dancers and bands significant but so were her song choices. With *Lemonade* having been released two years prior, she opted to perform songs from this album and others that speak to the Black experience. For example, "Freedom" was the second song she performed in her set. This was followed by "Lift Every Voice and Sing," which the National Association for the Advancement of Colored People (NAACP) declared the Black national anthem in 1919. The history of the song is rich, and its inclusion in the show is significant. The song was originally a poem written by NAACP leader James Weldon

Johnson in 1900. Later, the song was adopted by the NAACP and used as a rallying cry during the Civil Rights Movement of the 1950s and 1960s.[11] The choice of the song was noted with many on X declaring how happy they were to hear her sing it. When discussing these decisions and others, Beyoncé commented on the fact she has often been asked, "Why am I so insistent on giving them Blackness and Black culture?" before answering that she has no choice. She then goes on to argue that "we are the most beautiful people in the world," a message made front and center throughout this entire homecoming performance.[12]

This show was not just for the people who could afford a Coachella ticket. Beyoncé very deliberately made her performance accessible for those at home through a live stream and later with the release of her film on Netflix. As well as the show itself, the production of the film was executed with seamless transitions and shots of Beyoncé looking straight into the camera at many times. This was an even more important endeavor when you consider the history of gentrification at Coachella and its status as an expensive and predominately white festival. Given that those attending were likely to be white, as opposed to her community and core fan base, decisions like including the Black National Anthem were for us at home as well. The Black audience (there and at home) might find more connection to "Lift Every Voice and Sing" than white audiences in attendance (who were perhaps simply waiting for "Single Ladies"). Furthermore, she used the stage to showcase not only her work but the work of other hugely talented Black people, including contortionist-level dancers and trumpet players. It was especially important that she broadened the Black talent on stage given the subject matter. In a rejection of whiteness and elitism that is often associated with Coachella, Beyoncé brought Black people, Black culture, and Black history to one of the biggest stages in the world and then catapulted that stage into our living rooms.

Alongside the songs recorded from the performance, the *Homecoming* film and album also included Beyoncé's rendition of

"Before I Let Go," a cover of Frankie Beverly & Maze's 1981 smash hit. This cover quickly became a fan favorite with the inclusion of dance instructions in the chorus. The catchy beat and instructions in the lyrics inspired Fabron Alexis and Fred Barthell, dance instructors at Movez Dance Inc. to create simple but effective fun choreography to the song. Alexis posted a video on Instagram of him performing his choreography that was later shared by Beyoncé herself in one of her first-ever Instagram stories. This is how Beyoncé officially launched the #BeforeILetGoChallenge on social media. She posted the video alongside the hashtag and emojis, including her customary bee and heart-eyes emojis. She encouraged fans to submit their "Before I Let Go" videos and then shared their videos on her own platforms. The #BeforeILetGoChallenge grew and went global. It struck me that the communal joy shown throughout the entire Homecoming performance was on full display during the #BeforeILetGoChallenge as celebrities and fans alike attempted the challenge from across the globe. We were united.

After the Homecoming performance, there were many jokes about how Beyoncé created her own university with people taking to social media to pledge their allegiance to the BK sorority. As with every joke there is an element of truth, and upon reflection, in many ways she did create her own university—or at least a class or two. If there is a BK University, then the #BeforeILetGoChallenge is the official campus dance and chant. Ultimately, this movement was about more than the uniforms and dancing though; this university was about community and joy. For those of us used to having to pave our way and create our own spaces, she showed us how to do this and excel at the same time. More than that, she showed us how beautiful these spaces we create are and how much value they hold.

This show was undeniably about Beyoncé, to the point that many people still call Coachella "Beychella" years later, but it was also about Black culture. It was about how the African American community have time and time again created magic, and lemonade, out of whatever they have been given. As she said in the documentary, "we were able to create a free safe space where none of us were marginalized."[13] Much like at HBCUs, during the show Black people were prioritized and remained front and center, which is rare not just at Coachella but in America more widely. As Beyoncé said herself, "I wanted every person who has ever been dismissed because of the way they look to see themselves on that stage." And while this was a grand aim, I would argue it was certainly achieved. Beyoncé's decision to blend her personal narrative with a deep homage to Black culture created a stunning moment in pop culture. It was a celebration of Black colleges, Black pride, and Black excellence.

However, while discussing the historical significance of the references I can't neglect to mention what a masterpiece it was as a performance. The performance and film of it captures both the personal and the collective experience, making it a quintessential example of Beyoncé's ability to elevate the live performance to a space of elite social commentary. Those who cite Beyoncé as the greatest living entertainer use this Coachella performance as their number one argument. Everything from the vocals to the dancing was flawless, and this perfection is no surprise given the preparation and attention to detail we saw during the film. Luvvie Ajayi writes that during this performance especially, "we were watching a legend," and I whole heartedly agree.[14] As well as being undeniably culturally significant, Beychella was also one of the greatest live performances ever, and that combination was truly something to behold.

GOING GLOBAL

To be Black and alive in 2020 was to be irrevocably changed. That year, everyone was struggling, but Black people bore a disproportionate weight. From the murder of George Floyd in Minneapolis to the devastating impact the COVID-19 pandemic had on Black communities globally, it was a year marked by deep division and a painful, urgent need for connection. America has long avoided reckoning with its entrenched racial hierarchy, but I think the summer of 2020 brought it the closest it's ever come. It was a season of collective trauma—of televised deaths and mass protests, of grief and rage spilling into the streets. What I remember most from that time are the images: Black death replayed on my screens, day after day. And amid the chaos, the surreal detail of having food delivered to my doorstep by the chaotic UK government—sustenance arriving as the world around me unraveled.

Art exists in a context, and it was also at this turn of the decade that Beyoncé embarked on another ambitious multipart, multimedia project diving into the roots of her Blackness—this time honoring the artists and sounds of Africa. The two-prong project began with her album *The Lion King: The Gift*, a Beyoncé-led soundtrack to the 2019 remake of *The Lion King*, in which Beyoncé voiced the character Nala. This was followed by *BLACK IS*

KING in 2020, the Bey-conceptualized accompanying film that can only be called sonic cinema and the reason I finally caved and subscribed to Disney+. Beyoncé was integrating explicitly African work and sounds into her music prior to these projects. For example, her album *4* was influenced by legendary Nigerian bandleader and political activist Fela Kuti, who is regarded as the principal innovator of the Afrobeat music genre. As previously mentioned, Mozambican dance group Tofo Tofo also flew to the States to choreograph the video for "Run the World (Girls)." "Grown Woman," the bonus cut from her self-titled album, was also Afrobeat-inflected and featured striking vocals from Guinean singer and dancer Ismael "Bonfils" Kouyaté, whose chanting appears throughout and illuminates the song's bridge. *Lemonade* was also certainly different from anything we'd seen from Beyoncé before, and the imagery specifically drew from references from across the African continent.

However, *The Lion King: The Gift* took this a step further by showcasing not just the culture but the African continent itself. Afrobeat and Afropop leading lights like Mr Eazi, Burna Boy, Wizkid, Tiwa Savage, Shatta Wale, and Yemi Alade all featured on the album. While the album does consist of collaborations with giants like Pharrell, audiences also met lesser-known artists. Viewers were exposed to African elements ranging from Afrobeat (West Africa) and gqom (South Africa) to popular dance styles like the Network (Ghana) and Kpakujemu (Nigeria). Of course, Beyoncé did not popularize and certainly did not invent these genres. Music giants like Fela Kuti are always reaching new heights, and Afrobeat is and was a thriving genre of music, but Beyoncé's merging it with the world of American music and taking it to such a large audience was something new.

The Lion King: The Gift and *BLACK IS KING* were both a sumptuous display of African-derived fashion, style, art, and dance presented through the lens of a *Lion King*–esque story of a young African prince reclaiming his identity and his pride. Both projects engage with a culture that has been taken from African Americans. There are also visuals of landscapes across the continent, and the film shows the links between cultures and practices across the African continent and America, juxtaposing masks and durags, Johannesburg and Beyoncé's backyard. In doing so, and in telling the story of Simba, *BLACK IS KING* highlights the beauty of the collective Black diaspora. Interludes and dialogue from *The Lion King* film are also used throughout *BLACK IS KING* to follow Simba's journey, though in the album and film, he is represented as a Black boy rather than a lion. Importantly, Beyoncé is not on the cover of *The Lion King: The Gift* or *BLACK IS KING*, despite the fact that the film was partly written and directed by her. Instead, the cover for *BLACK IS KING* features the true star of the film's narrative, Simba himself, among the moon and stars.

The film follows Simba as he connects with his ancestors as well as his legacy and assuages temptation to step into his power. The entire project is a love letter to the African continent and a way of reclaiming African American links to this rich history and culture through the story of young Simba. We also see a man in blue paint throughout the film who also acts as a guide of sorts. In many African cultures, blue face paint holds symbolic significance, as it's often associated with peace, calmness, and affection. It's a color used in tribal art and ceremonies to convey messages, differentiate status, and connect with the spiritual realm. The specific meaning of blue can vary depending on the tribe and region, but its connection to the sky and divinity is common across different cultures. The image of the man in blue paint also references the blue used by some enslaved Africans to ward off hate.[1] And in Black American tradition, haint blue is a specific shade of blue-green used to paint porch ceilings to ward off evil spirts and ghosts. This practice has many ancestorial origins but is supposedly associated with the Gullah Geechee people, descendants of enslaved Africans in parts of Georgia and South Carolina, who have maintained a rich cultural heritage. Among their traditions was the belief that haint blue repels haints, or ghosts, who would be tricked into thinking that that "ceiling is water or the sky."[2] *BLACK IS KING* honors these diasporic connections, from these bright blue images to the scenic images of the Nile River.

The album and film open with the song "BIGGER" In this song Beyoncé as a spiritual guide instructs Simba to connect with his ancestors and decedents, to turn to the kings and queens. She urges Simba to step into his power and reclaim the crown that has been ripped from his head. This song seeks to remind Simba, and us all, that we are a part of something much bigger than ourselves; the song is essentially a series of affirmations. She tells him that he is more than just some words in a Bible verse, specifically rejecting how the Bible has often been weaponized against the Black community. As well as with these lyrics the film also contains many biblical references throughout, such as the story of Moses. Including these serves the purpose of rejecting the colonized version of Christianity that is often used against marginalized communities. The visuals present Black people as the true spiritual leaders.

These visuals subvert expectations of art history by switching between images of the Madonna, the Virgin Mary, and an Orisha during "BIGGER." These contrasting religious images highlight the whiteness and colonialism of Western Christianity within the global context. One tool of white supremacy and the American racial hierarchy is disconnecting African Americans from their heritage, be that clothing or music or spiritual practices, and it is this erasure that the film rejects by subverting these Western Christian images and reminding us of our greatness. What becomes clear is that with these songs and the message of the film, Beyoncé is not just addressing Simba; she is addressing all of us Black people. When she sings and ensures Simba that he is a king already, she is speaking to the entire diaspora. "BIGGER" essentially sets out the mission statement of the film, to explore how we are *all* gifts from the universe.

While *The Lion King: The Gift* is an album full of these uplifting messages, the Afrobeat-inspired song "DON'T JEALOUS ME" as well as the song "NILE" with Kendrick Lamar explore the darkest parts of human existence and the temptations Simba will face on his journey. "DON'T JEALOUS ME" features Tekno, Yemi Alade, Mr Eazi, and Lord Afrixana. The song uses multiple languages including Twi, Igbo, and Nigerian pidgin English, which is a language that combines a mix of dialects. The song follows Simba as he seeks his place and tribe. In "NILE," the major north-flowing river in northeastern Africa that is the title of the song is used as a metaphor for the African blood that runs through all of us, but especially African Americans. With these songs the film tells the story of the circle of life, inviting us to come home to ourselves but reminding us that this will not be an easy process. As well as following the narrative of the film and our Simba, the music and the interludes that accompany them also show us how traumatic events can deepen our roots and connections to who we are. *The Lion King: The Gift* is an album full of hard questions, and we really see Simba grapple with some of these dilemmas and temptations during "NILE" and as we continue to follow his sonic and visual journey.

During the *BLACK IS KING* film, there is a sample of a song by Solomon Linda. The song "The Lion Sleeps Tonight," which was originally called "Mbube," a title that refers to the Zulu word for lion, was written by Linda while he worked as a janitor in South Africa in the 1920s.[3] In the 1940s, Linda rose to fame in thanks to the song and his stunning soprano vocals. However, the song's long and complicated history was unfortunately not fair. In 1951, US folk singer Pete Seeger recorded a version with his band, the Weavers. In a predictable yet sad turn of events, with the four white voices signing the song, the looped chorus of "uyimbube" (which means "you are a lion" in Zulu) became "wimoweh," and the title of the Weavers' cover. After more people in the US became aware of the song, a doo-wop group named the Tokens added English lyrics to the song. This created the 1961 US number one hit "The Lion Sleeps Tonight," with Linda's name absent from the credits.

Three decades later the song continued to grow in popularity and became a centerpiece of Disney's animated classic *The Lion King*. Throughout this process the chorus was mispronounced, and English words steadily swapped the original beautiful Zulu lyrics. Also, despite the growth of the song's popularity, and while there is some debate around royalties, Linda was not fairly compensated for his talent. The song started an entire genre of music in South Africa, but the true importance of the song remains widely unknown. Linda continued to live in poverty, with one of his children even dying due to their impoverished circumstances. His descendants spent years seeking legal compensation. The inclusion of the Linda's version of the song in *BLACK IS KING* honors the African heritage of Simba while also highlighting how the West has consistently exploited and undervalued African art. Dr. Khalid Nas describes Beyoncé as a cultural archivist, and this is one moment in which I think she fully deserves this title.[4]

Another highlight in both the album and film is "MOOD 4 EVA." The song is led by Beyoncé, Jay-Z, and Childish Gambino, and features Malian Grammy winner Oumou Sangaré, who is often referred to as "the Songbird of Wassoulou." In this section of the film and album Simba battles temptations and the seduction of a carefree lifestyle, exactly as Simba does in the original *Lion King*. The title, "MOOD 4 EVA," is a contemporary play on the 1994 film's iconic phrase and song by the same name "hakuna matata," which means "no worries" in Swahili. This part of the film is a display of opulence and material wealth, with the music video for "MOOD 4 EVA" being shot in a mansion. In the video, Beyoncé wears pajamas with dollar signs printed on them and references the classic American film *Coming to America*, where Eddie Murphy plays a prince from a fictional African country called Zamunda. In a nod to the film, we see Beyoncé have a white butler brush her teeth for her. The video and Jay-Z's rap verse in the song also reference Mansa Musa, the richest person who ever lived and an African man during the Mali Empire.[5] It is easy to critique this display of wealth, especially from a celebrity like Beyoncé. However, I find the more important wealth in *BLACK IS KING* to be the culture and beauty on display.

In the context of the film, at this part of the story Simba is tempted by these simple pleasures and the sin-filled world of material wealth that he will ultimately reject. This clever subversion connects the continual references to diamonds throughout the album. Referencing diamonds is notable when one considers that over half of the world's diamonds are from the African continent.[6] For Black people who historically and continue to experience the displacement of natural resources and lack of financial stability through traditional generational wealth, we are uniquely situated to carry along our own form of wealth through culture and beauty. When watching this portion of the film, I am reminded that generational wealth can be applied to the culture we as Black people are lucky enough to have inherited, as well as the material wealth referenced in it.

As well as referencing Mansa Musa, Jay-Z's verse in "MOOD 4 EVA" also mentions Nipsey Hussle, a talented West Coast rapper who was known for his community work and his business ventures in clothing and music prior to his untimely death. Nipsey Hussle made it his life mission to not just achieve material success and wealth, but uplift his community in everything he did. Through his work we can see the true wealth of community that Nipsey Hussle made it his life's mission to support. The metaphorical crown that has been ripped from Simba in the film is as symbolic of this rich culture and history as it is about material wealth. So, while this song on the surface can seem like a grotesque display of opulence from two very rich celebrities, I personally find the wealth being celebrated here as cultural. Also, given generalized perceptions about the African continent, it is important that the video and film show that there are material wealth and valuable resources that have been historically stolen. Materially and culturally, the African continent is rich—and not in need of saving by the West.

"WATER," a song featuring Pharrell Williams and Cameroonian music executive Salatiel, echoes these themes and love letters to the continent as Simba continues his journey with the backdrop of a stunning coastline. Here water is symbolic of the natural beauty and resources that have historically been ripped from the African continent. The word "ashé," loosely translated to mean deep spiritual power or life in the Yoruba language, is repeated throughout this song.[7] "WATER" is about a deep, committed, and supportive love between the characters in the film and is a metaphor for adventure and devotion and for the beauty of the African continent. For me, this song encourages listeners to breathe and take in the beauty and impact of the album. This recognizable and unique song instantly took a deep place in my heart after one listen. As we learned with *Lemonade*, water can be a flood—but it can also cleanse, as it does in this song and in the story told by *BLACK IS KING*.

From exploring the natural beauty of Africa in "WATER," Beyoncé then moves on to exalting the beauty of Black women with perhaps the best-known song of the album, "BROWN SKIN GIRL." The song sees Beyoncé, Guyanese American R & B and hip-hop singer and rapper SaintJhn and Nigerian singer Wizkid sing about the beauty of dark skin tones. The song pays homage to West African music, passing the mic to groundbreaking artists with Afrobeat and dancehall backgrounds. It is important that Beyoncé, who has largely been accepted within the realms of Eurocentric beauty standards due to her lighter skin tone, celebrates the beauty of darker skin tones. This is especially important as colorism, the belief that light skin is preferable, still negatively impacts dark-skinned Black women and is used to divide the Black community. One song cannot undo centuries of prejudice, but in my opinion, it is important that Beyoncé fights against it. In addition to the household names featured on the song, Beyoncé's eldest child, Blue Ivy, sings on the track and is credited as an artist. She ends the song stating, in her very childlike and pure voice, that she wouldn't change anything about herself or any other

Black girl. This lyric is important due to critiques often leveled against her from a very young age pertaining to her appearance. Also, this lyric is the closest we will ever get to a direct comment from Beyoncé about the ridiculous commentary on her daughters' appearance. Other lyrics in the song also discuss the beauty of dark-skinned women like Kelly Rowland, Naomi Campbell, and Lupita Nyong'o, who also star in the video for the song. As with the artwork for the entire project, Beyoncé is not front and center for this video; instead she showcases the undeniable beauty of dark-skinned women and Black children.

In the song, Beyoncé sings about how she loves everything about these women, including their "nappy curls" by calling them the best thing in the world. The word "nappy" is often used negatively to describe textured hair, but the roots of the word in fact date back much further. Historians now believe that the origins of the term may originate from the arrival of the first slave ships in the seventeenth century.[8] The likely origin of the term is the word nap, which was used to describe the frizzled threads rising from a piece of cotton. However, there is much speculation that "nap" was redefined as a disparaging word for the coils and kinks in the hair of the African enslaved people in connection with the fields of cotton that drove the colonial economy. This reference is aligned with how the word is used today, often as an insult for those with coily or kinky hair. Beyoncé's use of the word nappy is purposeful in reclaiming it. The song is upbeat and uplifting with Wizkid and Saint Jhn's sounds providing a moment of celebration in the complicated story told by the album. I believe that among this celebration is where Simba starts intentionally championing and learning from the Black women around him.

As with most of Beyoncé's current discography, the video for "BROWN SKIN GIRL" adds meaning to the song. The video sees Black women and girls of many ages laughing and playing together, including Blue Ivy Carter. The video is a stunning celebration of Black beauty and Black womanhood. The costumes are a mix of Western and African clothing, representing the mixing of two cultures and the place Black women have in both. For this video, these women and girls represent beauty. The portion of the film when the song plays also focuses on Black girls as debutantes who take part in social competitions. These images of Black debutantes grow in importance when we remember how luxury and wealth and these ornate settings are usually attributed to whiteness. The women are dressed not just beautifully but regally, and the message is clear—each girl we see is worthy of the crown on her head. This is echoed in the lyrics with the comparison of their skin to the most valuable 24 karat gold. As the song continues, the dancers become less confined in their movements and begin having more fun with the music, even laughing. The video and the song also inspired the "BROWN SKIN GIRL" challenge on social media. Many used lyrics from the songs to caption images of themselves or many filmed themselves dancing to the song. This "challenge" attracted stars such as Black filmmaker Ava DuVernay and actress Lupita Nyong'o, with many parents also showing their children reacting to the lyrics. "BROWN SKIN GIRL" is the most child-friendly song on the album; the lyrics are wholesome and simple. This makes the song suitable for a Disney soundtrack and accessible to everyone with its uplifting message.

Two songs later, the message of *BLACK IS KING* is cemented with "ALREADY." Here audiences see dancers celebrate under the red, black, and green Pan-African flag, sometimes referred to as the Marcus Garvey flag.[9] Garvey was a Jamaican political activist and founder of the Universal Negro Improvement Association. Garvey aimed to achieve Black Nationalism specifically through the celebration of African history and culture, by and for all Black people. This in turn became symbolized by the Pan-African flag with its red, black, and green tricolor, representing the desired unity throughout the Black diaspora. The red stripe at the top of the flag represents the blood that unites all Black people and has been shed because of slavery and subjugation. The black stripe in the middle is a nod to Black people's skin color and serves to indicate the strength of their community. The bottom green stripe represents the fertility of the African continent and its natural richness and beauty. Showing this flag during a song that talks about how our power and greatness are already ours was an unapologetic statement of Black unity and Pan-Africanism. During the film when this song plays, this is where we see a romantic moment between Simba and Nala. The romance and the Pan-African references represent a theme of loving harmony among all Black people. "ALREADY" is an invitation to rule our own world and a reminder that we are, already, kings and queens without white and colonial validation. This message is further represented in the film by a Black man in a gold durag—a modern crown.

"MY POWER" with Beyoncé, Tierra Whack, Moonchild Sanelly, Nija, Busiswa, and Yemi Alade sees Simba, and all of us, fully step into our potential thanks to the guidance of Black women. The song sees these phenomenal female artists discuss their power and how it can never be taken. The lyrics make it clear that they are no longer waiting for a seat at the metaphorical table of power; they are making their own. At this part in *BLACK IS KING* Simba has begun to step into his power and begins to respect his crown in part due to the power and advice of Black women, just like in the original cartoon film when he returns home after seeing Nala. *MY POWER* sees all the women shine as they take turns to speak affirmations to themselves and each other. They gather around symbols of power and unity wearing red, the color of action and war.

There are many crucial references in Tierra Whack's verse especially. She urges listeners not to forget about Synclaire, Regine, and Maxine. The lyric is a reference to characters in the Black-cast sitcom *Living Single* that starred, among others, Queen Latifah. The record-breaking NBC sitcom *Friends* is said to be a white version of *Living Single*, with many using the latter sitcom to demonstrate that Black people "did it first" and did not get credit. *Friends* for many is an example of white American culture dominating at the expense of Black creativity, and the reference to *Living Single* in the song makes this point fantastically.

Tierra Whack further champions Black creativity by describing the language of Ebonics. Ebonics, or African American English, has its own grammar, vocabulary, and pronunciation, and is spoken by many Black Americans—particularly in urban communities. Despite the creativity of the language, it is often demonized and viewed as not significant. It has increasingly also been stolen or co-opted by white culture, with words like "slay" making their way into the public lexicon without credit given to the Black community that created them. When Black people use the word "slay", it's described as "ghetto," but it is accepted when spoken from white mouths. Tierra Whack referencing *Living Single* and Ebonics is a way of returning credit to Black creativity. Other lyrics in "MY POWER" discuss the way Christianity has been used against Black people and the entire African continent. Beyoncé invites Black people to reject the notion that African spirituality is "demonic" and step fully into their power. From Ebonics to colonized songs, Black culture has made the world turn, and *BLACK IS KING* seeks to give some of the credit where it is long due.

Lyrics from Nija are equally significant. She sings a chant that children from Kinshasa used to cheer on boxer Muhammad Ali during his famous "Rumble in the Jungle" fight against George Foreman. The chant, "Boma yé," means "kill him" in Lingala (one of the four recognized national languages in Democratic Republic of Congo). The choice to include an African dialect in "MY POWER" is important in reclaiming African American links to the continent, but this chant and the fight has a deeper meaning also. Muhammad Ali was a Black nationalist who was stripped of his medals for refusing to take part in the war in Vietnam. He was a member of the Nation of Islam and friends with civil rights leader Malcolm X. His medals may have been taken, but his power was not. More recently, when Blue Ivy joined Beyoncé on stage for her RENAISSANCE World Tour, it was this song she danced to. As the lyrics referenced kinfolk, Blue Ivy emerged on stage and began her dance routine. When discussing the meaning of this song, Beyoncé described the power of Blackness and how the song is an invitation for anyone to "get in your psyche and to make you feel like you're anything less than a king."[10] Given the critiques Blue Ivy has faced regarding her appearance from such a young age, the moment when she danced to a song about the power of Black womanhood and legacy was phenomenal. The film represented what many of us have known—Black women are a source of light despite the world's attempt to dim it.

BLACK IS KING is a story following the reimagined life of Simba, and rather than ending with a neat conclusion, it ends with a call to action for us all to continue the story and take the lessons with us. "SPIRIT" is one of the last songs of the album and the song that features most heavily in 2019 remake of *The Lion King*. It cleverly links gospel and the Black Church to the stunning ancestorial practices we have seen throughout the film as Beyoncé sings with a large Black gospel choir dressed in regal purple. When "SPIRIT" plays, this is the moment in the film where Simba finally returns home after following the guidance of the Orishas and his ancestors, again echoing the journey he takes in the original *Lion King* film. We also see Simba have a child of his own, completing the circle of life shown in the 2019 remake of *The Lion King* and in *The Lion King: The Gift* album. It is also at the end of the album that Beyoncé invites us all to join her Black parade.

Beyoncé, who we know is a fan of a surprise drop, released her song "BLACK PARADE" on June 19, 2020. Nothing is unintentional when it comes to Beyoncé's discography, and releasing the song on the nineteenth of June is no exception. The nineteenth of June is commonly known in the United States as Juneteenth, a holiday to celebrate the end of slavery. The nineteenth of June is reportedly the day the last slaves learned that the Civil War was over and that they had been granted freedom.[11] In the spirit of the holiday, which is usually celebrated with red food, the song is a joyful one. The song begins with celebratory horns alongside some rare home footage of Beyoncé with her son Sir Carter, to whom she dedicated the project. The song also embraces modern forms of African spirituality, as all of *BLACK IS KING* does, such as wearing all white to a funeral to symbolize renewal and a link to the spiritual realm. During the song she acknowledges the history Black people have with spirituality as the rulers of celestial lore while showing how these practices have developed throughout the diaspora. Beyoncé proudly talks about charging her crystals in the full moon, for example. These practices are also showcased in the film through the depictions of Christianity, such as images of the Virgin Mary.

Another lyric sees her claim that history is "herstory," again centering women in the narrative. She also states that being Black is a reason why "they" are always mad because being Black is enviable. Importantly, when discussing the enemy, the song uses the third-person pronoun "they" to represent white people that seek to uphold white supremacy. She subverts some of "their" tactics used against Black protestors, claiming that rubber bullets will simply bounce off her. Later in the song she gives a shout out to Tamika Mallory, who organized women's marches to protest the election of Donald J. Trump as president of the United States in 2016.[12] With her increasing platform Mallory implores us all to keep marching toward progress. Beyoncé invites us to be more like Mallory by making a picket line out of picket fences, instructing us to take symbols of white supremacy and use them for our protection. These lyrics and the figures Beyoncé calls upon make it clear that this "BLACK PARADE" is not just a song; it is a movement.

In "BLACK PARADE" Beyoncé also calls for reparations for Black Americans. Many in the Black diaspora and elsewhere believe African Americans are entitled to reparations for slavery and the historic injustices they have faced. In an article for *The Atlantic*, sociologist and activist Ta-Nehisi Coates laid out his case for reparations. He argues that America was built from unpaid labor from African Americans, and that they should be compensated.[13] It is not only activists who believe in this idea; recently Democratic candidates for president have also championed the idea that reparations are the only way to get rid of the toxicity and the economic gap caused by 250 years of slavery and a further 100 years of domestic terrorism.[14] Ironically, reparations for formerly enslaved people were agreed upon following the official end of slavery in the form of forty acres and a mule. Historians like Eric Foner often question how different America would look if this promise had been kept and the formerly enslaved had been compensated.[15] Importantly, Foner also reminds us that these "failed promises" still "reverberate today" and have had lasting consequences on American history.[16] However, despite this promise and the continued logical argument for reparations, this is still a contentious and radical issue for many. In fact, many believe the idea of reparations to be laughable or even dangerous. Beyoncé's explicit call in "BLACK PARADE" for reparations is perhaps the most radical lyric of hers to date.

Alongside the release of the song on Juneteenth, Beyoncé announced the creation of her BeyGood Black-Owned Business Impact Fund, which awarded grants to Black businesses impacted by COVID-19. Beyoncé then turned her website into a kind of Black parade, advertising many Black-owned businesses curated by her stylist Zerina Akers.[17] These themes are also present in the storyline in *BLACK IS KING* we have been following as we see Simba's victory lap after he finds his way back to his family and overcomes temptations. It is also our victory lap and an invitation to revel in our creativity and everything we have accomplished, despite all the forces that tried to prevent us from wearing our crowns.

My world felt so small in 2020, not only because I was living through several historical events but because I felt as if the world literally had shrunk to the size of my bedroom and local park. *BLACK IS KING* was needed, not only for the cultural elements and power, but also the space and beauty of its visuals. I needed to be anywhere but where I was, and that's what art can do—take me elsewhere. Systemic injustice continued, as did the pandemic, and being online as a Black person continued to be a unique kind of hard, but *BLACK IS KING* provided temporary escapism through visuals and messages I needed at that time. At the end of the film, Beyoncé thanks the entire Black diaspora across the globe for inspiring the world with their culture. This sums up what I believe *BLACK IS KING* and *The Lion King: The Gift* to be about: generational cultural wealth and Black unity throughout the diaspora, and the need to wake up from the myth of Western supremacy and wealth.

The film drew blowback for the perceived "Wakandafication" of Africa, the idea that the rich cultures of countries across Africa were homogenized to be more palatable to an American audience. More critique surfaced because there were not many East African references in the film, despite *The Lion King* films being set in Kenya. While my take is that the wealth referenced throughout *BLACK IS KING* means something deeper, it is also true that there are gross displays of capitalism unreachable to the vast majority of people shown throughout the film. If we are to discuss our beauty and glory, I agree money does not hold a place in that conversation. Burundian writer Judicaelle Irakoze wrote for *Essence* that we do not have to be associated with monarchy and manner to matter, and this is a valid critique of this project.[18] However, the film gained far more praise for its staggering visuals and deeply felt connection to the continent portrayed. In my opinion, African Americans trying to learn more about their roots to the continent is never going to be a seamless process. To reclaim African heritage is to reject the legacy and effects of slavery, whether that's proclaiming that Black *is* king, or wearing a dashiki.

Discussing the *BLACK IS KING* film and "BLACK PARADE" on *Good Morning America*, Beyoncé described how she wanted to shift the perception of the word Black. In the wake of a tumultuous year, she wanted to show how we as a people are rich in history, purpose, and lineage.[19] From "OTHERSIDE," an ode to bereaved Black mothers, to "BROWN SKIN GIRL," which championed our beauty, all the songs in the film and on the album seek to reclaim the power and heritage taken from so many of us. In *The Lion King: The Gift* and *BLACK IS KING*, Beyoncé embraces her African roots and celebrates multiple African cultures on a global stage. These bodies of work highlight not only African heritage from hairstyles to music but also critique the Western historical treatment of African people and their culture. An album is not going to counter colonialism, and as Beyoncé is not from the continent, the nuances of African culture are missed in her work, but I believe that *The Lion King: The Gift* should be viewed more as a celebration of the Black diaspora and Black wealth. Whether it was because of the context of 2020 when it was released or the stunning and warm images of the continent, I think it was impossible to sit down to watch *BLACK IS KING* without feeling emotional. This film and the album are odes to the power of African ancestry, wherever it has led you. To be Black is to be blessed and rich, and these two projects are a great reminder of that.

ACT III

WHY HER HARMONIES WERE MY FIRST THERAPY

BEYONCÉ AS A SOUNDTRACK TO HEARTBREAK AND HEALING

Like most people socialized as girls, I know what it is to try to contort myself into a version that will be adored. I know cheating. I know what it is to look at a phone and wait for a text message only to be greeted with a one-word response. I know what it is to sit on the floor of a room in college and cry, not fully knowing why, just knowing that I feel unlovable. I know what it is to hold on to words and tattoo them on my brain in the hopes that doing so will maintain some form of connection to the person who said them. I know what it is to hold my friend's hair back when she cries with grief over a social media update from an ex. I know what it is to cry with grief myself. Like most of us, I know what it is to completely lose myself in the pain and beauty of romantic love.

I remember one time, when it was especially bad. I sat in my room. I probably should have been writing an essay or doing something else that was expected of me, but I couldn't, I couldn't move. In that moment I did what I always do when emotions are not letting me live; I turned to music, Beyoncé specifically. It's no surprise that I, like so many, turned to Beyoncé in these moments of uncertainty. I didn't just turn to her because I enjoy her music; I chose to do so because a common theme of Beyoncé's work is an exploration of love and the pain of it. One aspect of her catalog that really strikes me is how she explores love of self and romantic love simultaneously. While she's known for anthems of empowerment, she has also written extensively about the vulnerability of love, heartbreak, and forgiveness, and I for one have really needed these songs.

When I listen to Beyoncé's music, I often think of the idea of separate spheres. While there are differences in what the notion of separate spheres means for women, essentially the idea exists to perpetuate the belief that we should avoid the domain of politics, paid work, commerce, and law. The patriarchal ideology of separate spheres is based primarily on notions of biologically determined gender roles and often justified by patriarchal religious doctrine. According to those who seek to uphold this separation, women's "proper sphere" is the realm of domestic life and is focused on childcare, housekeeping, and religion. While movements like the Enlightenment, the French Revolution, and the Civil Rights Movement helped spread the ideas of liberty, equality, and political rights, in practice such rights were often denied to women, who were seen as belonging to a different social sphere. Many feminist writers, such as the suffragists and civil rights icons like Ella Baker, have demanded political equality for women and provided searing criticisms of the "separate sphere" that confined women exclusively to the domestic space.[1] When Beyoncé speaks about being more than "just his little wife," she is rejecting this idea also.

When listening to Beyoncé I think of the idea of separate spheres but also how the personal sphere—the sphere of motherhood, love, and family—exists in the context of everything that is happening around our personal lives. Our ability to love is directly impacted by politics and work. We need to reject the idea of separate spheres not only because women should be able to occupy whatever position in society they wish to, but because these spheres are not separate at all. Love exists in a context, whether it is Eurocentric beauty standards or gendered expectations of what women should be. When Beyoncé sings a love ballad she is singing about so much more, because to love and be loved in a world that does not deem you worthy of such love is a radical act, and Beyoncé's work has always perfectly articulated that.

Beyoncé often used her work to discuss how political context and patriarchy impacts romantic love long before exploring these themes so expertly in *Lemonade*. For example, "If I Were a Boy" approaches how relationships (especially heterosexual ones) are rarely equal and are often very gendered in terms of the expectations on each partner. The lyrics see Beyoncé singing about what she would do if she was the man in the relationship. She ironically sings about how she would turn off her phone and essentially cheat on her hypothetical partner. The emotional high point of the song is when she discusses how the protagonist's wife will be waiting for him to come home while he continues to disrespect her. Beyoncé's music has broken a lot of rules, musically of course, but also in the portrayal of romantic love and how Black women are "supposed" to act in relationships. If broader popular culture is to be believed, we are supposed to "hold it down" the way the hypothetical wife in the song does. We are supposed to shoulder every burden and even protect the men who hurt us. The myth and expectation of the strong Black woman is most evident in interpersonal relationships, and songs such as "If I Were a Boy" turn these myths on their head and break the perception of Black women as unbreakable.

Beyoncé has consistently told us not to settle when it comes to relationships, a message that has been present in her work from the very beginning. Take for example the Destiny's Child song "Survivor." This hit is about not compromising yourself for romantic love and not losing sight of who you are and your own moral compass within heartbreak. "Bills, Bills, Bills" is another song about setting expectations and boundaries; granted these expectations are financial, but still—Black women deserve all the things. While these may simply sound like frivolous girl-empowerment "leave your man" anthems, they are radical. In a world that so often sees

Black women as romantically undesirable, it is important that we have these songs that demonstrate the high romantic expectations we can and should set for ourselves. "Irreplaceable," an undeniably huge hit in Beyoncé's catalog, sees her tell her man to leave because he was cheating. When Beyoncé tells him to pack his bags, it is an invitation to women to not expect anything less than what we deserve and to never forget our worth. Even in the most romantic songs on her albums, she invites listeners to prioritize themselves and this, unfortunately, is a reminder that I and many of my friends have needed.

A song I personally feel is underrated is "Ring Off," taken from an extended edition of her self-titled album. The song is dedicated to her mother, Tina Knowles, who went through a divorce after her father was unfaithful. It's an upbeat song, which given the subject matter may appear surprising, but it's about her mum recovering and finding herself again after the divorce. The song, as so much of her catalog does, rejects the traditional expectations of what a wife is and should be. The song ends with a clip of Tina Knowles talking about how she overcame the heartbreak, showing that we all need these reminders. The song "I Care," also on the self-titled album, comes to mind when I think about unreciprocated feelings and toxic relationships. It's an exploration of being hurt and undervalued in relationships, but also how we shouldn't let that harden us and change how we choose to love those in our lives.

Beyoncé's songs examine the issue of infidelity from many different angles, with songs like "Ring the Alarm" that embrace the anger and betrayal and with the *Lemonade* album that provides a long examination of infidelity in the context of Eurocentric beauty standards. An auntie of mine who was going through a divorce due to infidelity played *Lemonade* nonstop for months, not in chronological order, though, so I could tell how she was feeling based on what she was listening to that day. "Hold Up" represented the days where she was ready to redefine herself on her terms. Songs from the "Redemption" section of the album represented the days when she felt a deep longing. When I would hear Beyoncé singing "Sandcastles" in the background as I talked to her, I would know that wasn't a good day. *Lemonade* is often described as a therapeutic release, and I've seen firsthand from watching my auntie rebuild herself that this is so true. The album ultimately concludes with self-empowerment and reconciliation. Many bodies of work explore the pain of such situations, but I personally do not believe it has ever been explored with as much nuance before. I don't think I've even seen an artist so expertly explore the process of putting yourself back together. *Lemonade*, and indeed so many of Beyoncé's other songs, give us a template to heal and to feel. I am grateful for these songs, that my auntie had them when she needed them, and that so many women who know this kind of pain can play them loudly from their car speakers, finding some comfort in the fact that they are not alone in these emotions.

Writer and African American studies scholar Daphne Brooks writes that Beyoncé's music encourages Black women especially to "take a deep breath."[2] While songs such as "I Care" have given me space to cry over a bad date or unread text message, songs such as "Dangerously in Love 2" also afforded me the space to revel in the softness of love. Yes, Beyoncé does sing about cheating and bugaboos, but she also makes songs about the beauty and necessity and healing nature of healthy romantic love. These songs tell us we are desirable and that we *should* expect love. "PLASTIC OFF THE SOFA," "LEVII'S JEANS," and "Sandcastles" demonstrate that love is important and necessary for all our journeys. We speak about how Black women are often denied the freedom to be angry and to be their authentic selves, whatever that may be, and the same can be said about their expression of positive emotions too. It is for these reasons I find the way Beyoncé sings about the softness of love incredibly validating and equally important.

"Dangerously in Love 2," the title song from her first studio album reminds us that romantic love can bring out a softness in us, as well as the more intense negative emotions. As a child, I sang this song in my bedroom, enamored by a crush that I was certain I would end up marrying. It goes without saying that there were also Beyoncé ballads playing when I married my wife in 2022. In both moments what I was listening to was more than love songs; these songs gave me permission to hold out for the kind of love I truly wanted. While I have, at times, settled for love that is not worthy, I have always had these songs to remind me that I do deserve to be held in every sense of the word.

In 2018 Beyoncé and Jay-Z released *EVERYTHING IS LOVE* just two years after the release of *Lemonade* and one year after Jay-Z's *4:44*. This joint album follows the revelations shared in *Lemonade* and *4:44* to conclude the story, or at least the parts of the story they both decided to share. The album cover's artwork is of a Black woman in a beige bodysuit combing a Black man's hair as he looks straight into the camera. The themes of the album are romantic love and partnership, but even more importantly self-love. *Lemonade* and *4:44* explore how love for a Black couple exists despite and in opposition to the American racial hierarchy, and *EVERYTHING IS LOVE* continues these themes. Often artistic bodies of work explore romantic love as if it exists in its own orbit, as if it can somehow escape the context of the world. These three bodies of work expertly detail how love, like everything, exists in the context of the world around it.

The song "BLACK EFFECT" from *EVERYTHING IS LOVE* opens with Jamaican author and dancer Lenora Antoinette Stines. The introduction of the song has since been the subject of a legal battle between the Carters and Stines due to a reported lack of permission to use the sample.[3] We hear Stines discuss the beauty and all-encompassing nature of love, which is the thesis of the album. Jay-Z then begins the chorus, speaking about how he is good on any Martin Luther King–named boulevard. Streets named after the civil rights icon are most common in Black American neighborhoods, such as the Martin Luther King Blvd. in South Los Angeles. Jay-Z's lyric emphasizes that he is most comfortable around his community. It is important to note that Jay-Z has constantly been critiqued on his appearance, and many of the songs on the album address these critiques. Jay-Z's verse is about loving himself, including his hair, which he wears in locs with "no perm in it." In his rap he also compares himself to Malcolm X, a figure well referenced in Beyoncé's work. He then tells listeners that he is even Blacker than the Essence Festival. The Essence Festival is the largest African American cultural and music event in the United States held annually in New Orleans. These lyrics see Jay-Z proudly claim his Blackness as a beautiful thing to be celebrated, and given the way in which Jay-Z has been called ugly for his African features, this celebration is very significant.

The album argues that Black love is a rejection of white Eurocentric beauty standards. One lyric sees Beyoncé state that she will not let people shoot the nose "off my pharaoh." This line continues the theme of Pan-Africanism in her most recent work, while proclaiming that she loves her partner's Black features, a point she also made during "Formation." Beyoncé continues to love Black bodies by identifying with Sarah Baartman's hips, hips that she describes as beautiful. Sarah Baartman (otherwise known as Saartjie Baartman) was born in the Eastern Cape province of South Africa. Scottish scholar Alexander Dunlop brought Baartman to London to exhibit her body in a freak show under the name Hottentot Venus in 1810. Culture writer Jaelani Turner-Williams describes how "along with being exhibited at London's Piccadilly Circus, Baartman could also be displayed for private exhibitions, where viewers could touch her without consent."[4] The life of Sarah Baartman has come to represent the objectification and sexualized fascination with the Black female body. Beyoncé, by referencing her life, reclaims features that have often been used to define and degrade Black women. In *Lemonade*, Beyoncé positions police brutality as another force that seeks to undermine Black love. Brittney Cooper, founding director of the Race and Gender Equity Lab at Rutgers University, states, "Beyoncé named the pain of a whole generation of Black women who have had to love Black men injured and traumatized by the ravages of Reaganomics, the prison industrial complex, and the war on drugs."[5] Black love is more than simply relationships or a hashtag; it's a tool in the fight against white supremacy.

"APESHIT," a song on *EVERYTHING IS LOVE*, sees Beyoncé and Jay-Z sing and rap about their lavish lifestyle. The song was produced by Pharrell Williams and features rapper Quavo. On the surface there is very little politically progressive about this song. It is somewhat of a capitalist anthem, with the Carters bragging about their status and skill. However, the video adds meaning with its sharp commentary about power and Eurocentric beauty standards. In the video Beyoncé, Jay-Z, and a team of dancers take over the famous Louvre Museum in Paris, the home of the *Mona Lisa*.[6] Many online were gushing over (and laughing about) the fact that Beyoncé "bought out" the Louvre Museum for the video, speculating on the cost of doing so. This act was a display of wealth and power in keeping with the lyrics of the song, and later in the song they both stand in power suits with their backs to the *Mona Lisa* and look directly into camera. This image makes me question what society considers to be beautiful and worthy of admiration. Through the song and the visuals, the pair provide an alternative meaning of power, opulence, and beauty. In the song Jay-Z calls himself a gorilla. Unfortunately, the words "gorilla" and "monkey" are insults often leveled against Black people. However, the lyrics turn the insult on its head and describe the power and majesty of the gorilla. Completely subverting this insult and finding power matches the intention behind the entire album. Including and lyrically subverting this insult highlights that Eurocentric beauty standards impact Black men as well as Black women. In this song, they also reject the establishment that has never validated or championed Black art.

"APESHIT" also explores the complicated relationships Black artists have with establishments more broadly. In his lyrics Jay-Z references rejecting the opportunity to perform at the Super Bowl halftime show out of solidarity for Colin Kaepernick, an

American quarterback who has a long history of protesting police brutality and racial inequality, sacrificing his football career to do so. Jay-Z goes on to express a level of contempt for the Recording Academy. In 2018, Jay-Z was nominated for eight awards at the 60th Annual Grammy Awards, including Record of the Year for "The Story of O.J.," Song of the Year for "4:44," and Album of the Year for *4:44*. He was awarded none of them. In "APESHIT," Jay-Z disregards the establishments that have a history of disrespecting Black Americans, instead stating that their power does not come from white people or industry validation. The hook of the song sees the duo stating that the crowd's support at their concerts is all the validation they need. True to the spirit of this lyric, in her latest work Beyoncé's appears increasingly free in her output, focusing more on her art and the response from her audience, rather than establishment support. Throughout her career, Beyoncé has been devalued by the establishment. So, seeing her and Jay-Z seemingly ignore these industry accolades and turn to each other and their community instead is, to me at least, empowering.

The references to their lifestyle and wealth in *EVERYTHING IS LOVE*, and their domination of the Louvre, further cements Beyoncé and Jay-Z's status as a power couple. While the idea that liberation and power can be found in such opulence is contentious, I feel there is a more significant point to the album—love. The album is at its core about how their love overcame the obstacles they have both discussed previously, obstacles they attribute to white supremacy. The final song on the album is "LOVEHAPPY" and reveals more details about their relationship, including that they decided to get remarried. The song and album end with a statement about how they are happy in love, and this love is how they conquered it all.

Those who know her music know that every Beyoncé album tells a story, and love is a key theme in all of them. Romantic love is not absent from the glittery ballrooms of *RENAISSANCE*, and it is in *COWBOY CARTER* as Beyoncé reclaims country music.

Albums like *Lemonade* also beautifully illustrate that love is not separate from her experience as a Black woman. As sociologist Maria Brito states, "Every woman who has ever felt mad, betrayed, angry, invalidated, cheated, vengeful, obsessed, or brokenhearted finds catharsis in Beyoncé's music."[7] This is because in her music, she explores the multidimensional way women exist in love as well as all our emotions and our sexuality. By prioritizing and giving space for these emotions her music offers a journey of self-healing and empowerment.

At my wedding my wife and I danced to "Love on Top." On reflection, this song does not really represent our story. Having thoroughly examined the lyrics I personally do not know why the narrator of the song did not leave the clearly toxic and nonreciprocal relationship she sings about before she was "finally" loved back. On that day, as I said my marriage vows in front of people I adore and guests I didn't know as well, I found strength in showing them the most emotional part of me. As I danced to this song and other classic Beyoncé love ballads on my wedding day, it struck me that she really has provided the soundtrack to my romantic life. Not only the portion of it when I cried in my college dorm room, but the portion that is filled with the happy times too. There have been times I forgot my self-worth, times when I have been heartbroken, and times when love finally made sense and I learned what true partnership is.

Not only has Beyoncé's music provided the soundtrack for my own love story, but it has also helped me learn and understand what I want and what I deserve. A lot of work and support got me to this point of true love: therapy, time, and the gift of aging are all to be thanked, but so is Beyoncé's work. I am of the belief that we all need a soundtrack to understand our romantic relationships and feelings; for me, this soundtrack has been gifted by Beyoncé. She's seen me cry over a college boyfriend and later hitch my wedding dress up so I could dance with my wife. Beyoncé's ballads have made so much more sense to me since meeting the woman who would become my wife, but Beyoncé has also given me the courage to leave after being cheated on and to recognize the upbeat instrumental of true love when it does arrive. While I am grateful to her discography for so much, I feel like love can bring out the rawest version of us all, and it is in these moments where I personally feel as though I have really needed the music.

EIGHT REASONS WHY I CRIED AT THE RENAISSANCE WORLD TOUR

(I) Because of my fellow attendees.

I have long been of the belief that something very special happens when queer people gather to dance and are afforded the simple freedom of being able to move our bodies. After attending the RENAISSANCE World Tour (twice), I feel this is no longer a belief. It is now a fact as I have proof. While the show itself was phenomenal, the enormity of what Beyoncé had created became clear long before the music started. The beauty of the stage and set struck me as I walked up to the arena among a sea of rainbow fans, bedazzled cowboy hats, and sequins (I really cannot over-exaggerate the number of sequins there were). As people posed outside the stadium for photos, looking directly into their friends' cameras, it became evident to me that these arenas had become places for self-expression—and photoshoots. There was something unique about entering this space that had more-than-the-normal concert excitement. After looking back, I realize now it was the people. It was the people that turned the concrete wastelands outside the stadium into *the* place to be, and this is why I will always be grateful for everyone who was in the stadium when I saw Beyoncé perform during the RENAISSANCE World Tour.

If the line to get in was an event, seeing the stage itself was indescribable. The very first thing we saw was a huge disco ball above the sage in the colors of the Pride flag, and at every stage of this tour the queer community was front and center. Entertainment architectural team Stufish writes that "The expansive stage architecture evokes the feminine and futuristic disco feel of the *RENAISSANCE* era, with a curved main stage that extends into a circular catwalk embracing the pulsing Club Renaissance at the center of the stadium."[1] The couple next to my friend and I leaned back over their seats to try to get a photo of them kissing in front of the giant disco ball, and when I remember the tour it is this moment that has stuck in my head most. I remember Beyoncé being her own opening act, and I can still picture the stunning outfits (including the famous bedazzled Loewe bodysuit with glittering manicured hands printed on it) and her phenomenal vocals, but the open queerness of that kiss is cemented in my memory. Seeing these two people not feel any trepidation about being who they are exemplified to me what this album and tour was about—queerness on the stage. For those two hours of the concert, I did not care how others saw me, only how I saw myself. There was something about being in the sea of sequins that made me feel a part of a crowd in the best way. I was seen but not judged, and that is so unique. With the RENAISSANCE World Tour, Beyoncé created a space where her fans could be authentically themselves. This is the power of a truly great performance, to make the audience forget to code switch and forget themselves in a sea of glamour and power ballads.

(2) Because she dedicated the album to her Uncle Johnny.

Beyoncé has spoken about her late cousin, known as Uncle Johnny, publicly many times. When accepting her GLAAD Media Award in 2019, she lovingly refers to him as "the most fabulous gay man" and declared that witnessing his struggle with HIV was one of the most painful experiences of her life.[2] Beyoncé wrote in a dedication for *RENAISSANCE* not just about him but about "all of the fallen angels whose contributions have gone unrecognized for far too long."[3] However it was not just the dedication that honored this community, but the unabashed joy in the entire project. Even while sharing the story of her Uncle Johnny, she did not focus on queer suffering or oppression. During the tour and on the album there were no news reports with queer faces on them, no stories of how we had to throw bricks and then dig ourselves out of concrete—there was just our art, the most beautiful of tributes. Both the tour and album turned a tragic loss of a loved one into a celebration of Black queer fashion, joy, and dance—and it was something to behold.

Every Beyoncé performance is truly unique, but I have never seen anything like the two shows of the RENAISSANCE World Tour. Both the tour and album mean so much more when you realize they are a tribute. The whole project was the campest thing I have ever seen in my life, and the most joyous. I, the person next to me, and the person next to them all had rainbow fans and attempted fan choreography during "HEATED." We failed at said fan chorography; it's hard. There were couples holding hands, friends dancing with each other. The attendees and the show itself created a space of total joy and sparkle, and what a perfect way to remember all the fallen angels, what a perfect tribute. The last thing the audience saw of the show was a picture of Beyoncé's Uncle Johnny blown up large enough for thousands to see. While the tour was a love letter to the Black queer community more broadly, this celebration of her Uncle Johnny specifically made this global and larger-than-life event also feel so personal, and I am very grateful to have borne witness.

(3) Because Black queer music is a special kind of magic.

To understand why and how the RENAISSANCE World Tour became the best of gay clubs, you must understand how the album itself is a love letter to the Black queer community and their artistic output. The album takes inspiration from the house music scene, which has its roots in largely Black queer clubs like Chicago's legendary Warehouse, which was founded in 1977. *RENAISSANCE* also features the New Orleans bounce sound of regular Beyoncé collaborator and non-binary icon Big Freedia. As mentioned, Big Freedia is a rapper known most for her work in bounce music and bringing this genre to the mainstream, so hearing this voice embedded in the album and tour was important. The iconic collaborations and samples in both the tour and the album are almost countless. Ts Madison is another example of a sampled queer icon for the album. With her reality show, *The Ts Madison Experience*, she became the first Black transgender woman to star in and act as executive producer of her own reality series. On the album, we also hear trailblazing trans DJ and musician Honey Dijon. Honey Dijon serves as the lead producer on two *RENAISSANCE* tracks: "COZY" and "ALIEN SUPERSTAR." Because Beyoncé was clearly playing a game of let's make this album as queer as possible, "ALIEN SUPERSTAR" also samples the 1991 song "I'm Too Sexy" by Right Said Fred, an English band founded in 1989. This cheeky song is largely known as a gay anthem and fits in well with *RENAISSANCE*.

The tribute to queer culture doesn't stop there; in a moment that is a highlight of the album, Grace Jones is also referenced and featured on the song "MOVE." While not speaking publicly on her sexuality, Grace Jones is known among the queer community as an icon due to her breaking of the gender binary in terms of her appearance and artistic output. Another great moment comes in the song "PURE/HONEY" that samples "Miss Honey," the sleeper hit performed by Moi Renée. Moi Renée is a legendary Jamaican drag queen who was known in the underground queer scene for their high camp performances at New York venues such as The Shelter and Midtown 43. Since its release in 1992, "Miss Honey" has remained a staple within LGBTQ+ spaces. The musical stylings of Kevin Aviance, a member of the House of Aviance (one of the United States' major vogue-ball houses), is also honored with a sample of his hit "Cunty." With this sample and others, *RENAISSANCE* also embraces and uses the vernacular of ballroom culture.

Throughout the album, queer culture was not taken; it was embraced and platformed. From the samples to the artists she worked with, the entire album was a celebration of the queer community. With this album and these collaborations, Beyoncé seeks to correct the erasure of Black cultural production within these genres. For too long Black queer creativity has been stolen and monetized by white artists. With the album and tour, Beyoncé instead collaborated with numerous Black queer pioneers and placed them in their rightful place—on the world stage. It is important to note that Beyoncé has explicitly given her support to the queer community many times prior. For example, in a virtual ceremony for graduates in 2020, Beyoncé explicitly told them that their queerness was beautiful.[4] Also, her video for "7/11" referenced Pride parades.[5] However, the RENAISSANCE World Tour took this message much further, from the genres she reclaimed to the gender-neutral bathrooms available at performance venues. Sure, she did reclaim house and disco, but she also placed the Black queer pioneers of the genres front and center of this reclamation.

(4) Because she turned her stage into a ball.

If we are talking about Black queer creativity, then ball culture must be at the front of the conversation. Ball culture has gone through many evolutions, from previously enslaved people hosting drag balls, to the integrated vibrant drag balls that brought life to cities such as Chicago and New York. During these balls, Black and Latinx attendees could "walk" a category for prizes as well as for trophies. Balls were more than dances, more than a celebration of beauty; balls were a direct response to marginalization. They were a way for these communities to create a place where the only people judging them were each other, where they could exist on their own terms. They could wear what they want and dance how they want. However, with drag and ball cultures' momentous leap into the mainstream, Black people have increasingly become pushed out of the culture they created. Ball culture was for and by Black queer people. You cannot (or rather should not) celebrate this rich and fun part of LGBTQ+ culture without acknowledging this history.

Beyoncé replicated a ball on the RENAISSANCE World Tour. On multiple occasions during each show she left the stage, and her dancers, the vast majority of whom were Black and visibly queer, took ownership of it, walking it like a runway, voguing, twerking, and having a literal mini ball. It is essential to note that Beyoncé was not on the stage when this happened. Whether or not this was for a costume change or another practical reason, the result is that the dancers were placed front and center to reclaim their culture.

Fans, myself included, have been asking Beyoncé for the *RENAISSANCE* visuals (music videos, a film—at this point we'd take a photoshoot) since the album's release. With the futuristic, queer bounce-inspired vibe of the album, we believe that the music videos or a *Lemonade*-style film would be stunning. This desire led to fans attending shows in the RENAISSANCE World Tour with signs asking, "where are the visuals?"' One night on tour Beyoncé famously gestured to the crowd and finally replied, "You are the visuals, baby."[6] Though a comedic moment for those of us desperate for said visuals, her statement also highlighted her intent with the album, the tour, and the ball. It was to shine a light on her fans, specifically her Black queer fans. For so long we *have* been the visuals, and it is about time we were seen.

(5) Because of the clothes.

One of my key memories from the two shows I attended on the RENAISSANCE World Tour was seeing Beyoncé be her own opening act in a stunning ball gown, a different stunning ball gown every night to be exact, performing a stripped-down, almost acoustic version of some of her iconic ballads. It turns out that

Beyoncé singing a rendition of Mary J. Blige's "I'm Goin' Down" in a floor-length gown before sitting on a grand white piano is gorgeously camp. I don't know how Beyoncé singing a ballad about a man in a ball gown is gay; I'm just here to tell you that it was. One of Beyoncé's most famous recent lyrics, and one that was shouted by everyone in the audience of each performance in the RENAISSANCE World Tour, is when she brags about how her Uncle Johnny crafted her dress. This is more than a statement about a garment; it is a testament to how current popular culture is designed by queer Black people and countless queer Black people like him made so much that they never received credit for.

As referenced in "HEATED," her Uncle Johnny designed many of Beyoncé's early outfits and is credited with instilling in her and her sister a love of fashion. Beyoncé wore 148 costumes over the tour's run, many of which honored local designers at each stop of the tour, including Jacquemus in Marseille, Robert Wun in London, Stella McCartney in London and Barcelona, and Iris van Herpen in Amsterdam.[7] She opened each show singing ballads in ball gowns, which led to a fun game on social media where people would post what Beyoncé gown they got to see in person. For the June 18 show in Amsterdam, Beyoncé celebrated the Juneteenth holiday by wearing exclusively Black designers, including Feben, Maximilian Davis for Ferragamo, Olivier Rousteing for Balmain, and IB Kamara for Off-White, as well as her own Adidas x Ivy Park collection of course. The outfits were art, and as the best art does, they told a story. From her Uncle Johnny making a young Beyoncé her outfits, to the designers she wore on stage for the RENAISSANCE World Tour, in this context clothes were more than just fashion. So yes, this intentionality and attention to detail meant that clothes made me cry.

(6) Because I could see myself in the past.

I'm a historian by trade, and as such I am obsessed with the past. In doing this work I have realized that people, and by that, I mean certain people, and by that, I mean certain white people, often can't imagine Black or queer people in the past. The truth is we *were* always here, and it really isn't hard to see us if you want to. But I do admit they don't make it easy. Images of us taken in color are converted to black and white, and Black history is taught as if it began on slave ships. This revisioning and erasure is intentional and creates the perception that we as a people are new. It becomes hard to cut down a tree when you have knowledge of how deep its roots are. Beyoncé stated for *Harper's Bazaar* that "I think we are all ready to escape, travel, love, and laugh again. I feel a renaissance emerging, and I want to be part of nurturing that escape in any way possible."[8] This general concept of a renaissance and the references to the Renaissance of the fifteenth and sixteenth centuries meant that I knew themes of time would be strong in the album and tour. I still was not quite prepared for Beyoncé to recreate Sandro Botticelli's painting *The Birth of Venus* by emerging from inside a giant shell to sing "VIRGO'S GROOVE." Everything she does is intentional, and performing "VIRGO'S GROOVE," one of the slower and more sensual songs on the album, while turning herself into a live version of a painting that symbolizes love, birth, and spiritual beauty is suitably layered. It is worth noting that this is not the first time Beyoncé, an art collector and lover of art history, has referenced classic paintings. For example, in the video for "Mine" she references the surrealist René Magritte's painting *The Lovers* from 1928.[9] But, as you may expect from the name of her tour and album, she took these references to the next level. To many people, Beyoncé referencing an old painting may not seem particularly interesting in a show where she flew over our heads on a giant model horse that fans named Reneigh. But seeing her put herself, and by extension us all, in the past where we were turned into black and white was quite wonderful.

(7) Because I could see myself in the future.

One of the earlier tracks on the album is "ALIEN SUPERSTAR." In the lyrics Beyoncé discusses how she's so elegant and classy, that she is metaphorically out of this world with a futurist sound helped by stacked vocals that continue in the rest of the album and the tour. On the tour, the backdrop to the stage was a giant screen with a large "portal" in its center and featured sculptures, robotic arms, and ultraviolet technology. During one of my favorite moments of the tour, she danced with a robot. This was not like a cute two-step they danced; it was a full-on choreography. The imagery and dystopian futuristic alien visuals in between the costume changes were also something to behold. These interludes, if you can even call them that, referenced fashion and art history to tell a story. One visual interlude showed a perfectly maximalist montage of intergalactic travel and robotic machines. This robot-themed segment of the show was interspersed with spoken-word voice-overs from legendary ball commentator and music producer Kevin Jz Prodigy in yet another homage to ballroom culture. It struck me that many of these images would belong in a classic sci-fi film (if sci-fi films were not overwhelmingly white, of course). The show was intentional and brilliantly crafted from start to finish, the futuristic robot dancing included. Not to be hyperbolic, but seeing images of Black queer people in space felt very healing to me. These moments and the references to the Renaissance period created a beautiful combination of putting gay people in the future while also creating space for us in the past. The queer past and future coexisted so wonderfully on this stage, so I hope you can see how this made me cry.

(8) Because the entire tour had me thinking a lot about space.

I thought about not just the alien-robot-dancing kind of space, but spaces in general. The biggest questions I left the two shows I attended with (other than, how can I afford to go again?) were: What does it mean to not only exist in but to dominate a space? What does the world look like when the marginalized create the social norms, when hot pants and fan choreography are not only tolerated but mandatory? When people discuss icons for gay communities, like Mariah Carey, Madonna, and Kylie Minogue, I often find Beyoncé is neglected from these conversations. I believe this is because she caters to gay people of color. I, like many queer Black people, am aware of what it is to shape-shift. I know what it feels like to desire a neon makeup palate but worry about what a hypothetical stranger might think, to enjoy dancing at a party but make sure my waist doesn't move too much. The queer community is often associated with flamboyance, but truthfully most of us exist day by day as shells of ourselves. We navigate pronouns in our head and modify our wardrobe as literal and metaphorical voices tell us to shape-shift, but the RENAISSANCE World Tour provided a space where this code-switching was unnecessary. In *Renaissance: A Film by Beyoncé*, the tour documentary, Beyoncé told us that her goal with this tour was not perfection. Instead, she focused on joy and existing, and offering her audience the space to do the same, to exist as authentic versions of themselves.[10]

I have long held the belief that joy is protest, and after the RENAISSANCE World Tour, I have proof. The album *RENAISSANCE* was supposed to be released after *COWBOY CARTER*, but after numerous COVID-19 lockdowns and the start of a second Trump presidency, Beyoncé decided that we needed a release. Essentially—we needed a party. The timing was perfect. *RENAISSANCE* exemplifies the necessity of art to create sanctuary and connection in a world that can strip us of both so easily. On the bus back from her show in Cardiff, I turned to my dear friend and we came to the unspoken but inevitable agreement that we were going to buy more tickets and go again. This (expensive) decision fulfilled a need for more freedom, more minutes of release, more mandatory hot pants, and more dancing. I gained core memories and invaluable lessons from the RENAISSANCE World Tour as I'm sure all attendees did, but, most importantly, I made a vow to never shape-shift again and instead to force my body to do nothing but express unabashed joy.

AN ODE TO THE CONTRADICTION OF "CHURCH GIRL" AND THE BEAUTY OF VOODOO

In her song "CHURCH GIRL" Beyoncé mixes gospel with the unmistakable sounds of hip-hop and New Orleans bounce music. The song samples the African American gospel group the Clark Sisters, often called the First Ladies of Gospel, as well as bounce legend DJ Jimi. Traditionally, these genres differ in tone, beat, and execution and would perhaps contradict each other or clash. On the surface, a gospel sample does not belong next to up-tempo bounce-inspired lyrics and beats. However, in "CHURCH GIRL," these sounds do not clash. In fact, I would argue they work in perfect harmony. During the song, the gospel-inspired sections frequently shift into the fast-paced bounce beat. The combination of these sounds produces a catchy song that is part gospel and part dance tack. The result feels like the musical equivalent of removing a long coat when you get into a club or party, shedding inhibitions and the outside world in order to dance. As the song develops, we see that this contrast of genres and sounds is symbolic of the clashing expectations frequently placed on Black women, specifically to be both the prayer and the party. Sonically and lyrically "CHURCH GIRL" is a musical description of the endless cycle of sin and forgiveness that is the human experience.

Outside of the musical references and samples, even the lyrics are a love letter to Black women, who are frequently tasked with being all things to all people.

To understand the themes in "CHURCH GIRL," an awareness of the rich history of the Black Church in America must be acknowledged. The Black Church is integral to Black life as well as the Civil Rights Movement and liberation struggles. It was established by free and enslaved African Americans in search of spiritual liberation. Later, the Black Church would prove instrumental in the struggle for liberation and combating the evils of Jim Crow segregation. During the Civil Rights Movement African Americans convened at churches to organize and plan as well as to pray. Churches have been not only a site of praise for so many but a site of salvation and liberation also. Many prominent African American leaders have attributed their success to the church and were pastors themselves, Martin Luther King Jr. being one of the key examples. One cannot deny how integral the church has been, and is still, to African American life.

Beyoncé grew up in a Methodist church, attending St. John's United Methodist Church in Houston. She has said that gospel is the "most powerful type of music" and music is integral to worship and praise.[1] When analyzing how Beyoncé discusses spirituality and religion within her music it is important to remember these themes have been present in her work since the start of her career. Her girl group was, after all, called Destiny's Child in reference to the Book of Isaiah and reportedly chosen by Tina Knowles. Beyoncé has also often used her music to discuss the coexistence of Christianity and sexually liberated feminism and independence. One example of this can be seen in the video for "Survivor" by Destiny's Child.[2] The video follows the three bandmates as they wake up on a desert island in fabulous and minimal clothing and then plot and execute their escape. The video also sees Beyoncé sing about how she will not let a man reduce her to compromising her commitment to Christianity. This lyric is accompanied by a close-up shot of Beyoncé's legs in short shorts.

This is one of the first times we see her explore her faith in her work at the same time as she explores her sexuality.

What is clear is that while there is love, freedom, and community in all churches, there can also be judgment, particularly toward young women and sex. Ultimately, church girls are expected to be respectable. Skirts must be of a proper length; there is to be no looseness. The kind of sexuality Beyoncé embraces in songs like "Naughty Girl" and "Get Me Bodied" on the surface appear to be the anthesis of what should be expected from a church girl. In fact, far from just being discouraged, embracing female sexuality is often punished in some religious settings. The Black Church, like nearly all religious institutions, has often had a complex and negative relationship with sexuality, and this institution that has been so integral in the fight for freedom has sometimes perpetrated its own forms of oppression for women raised in these environments. Conservative churches especially have for too long taught women that their bodies are temples, but for visitors not of their choosing. The Black Church has undeniably done so much good, but the respectability politics it can perpetuate has very often been damaging for Black women.

It soon becomes clear when listening to "CHURCH GIRL" that this song is an invitation to dance away the shame associated with our bodies and how we use them. The lyrics see Beyoncé describe church girls as being naughty, despite the fact they will go to church in the morning. But rather than being a punishment or an insult, the song is an ode to that naughtiness. And why not? Why not feel pride in who you are on a Saturday night as well as who you are on a Sunday morning? We are nothing if not a summary of all our days and all our decisions, and "CHURCH GIRL" invites listeners to embrace the fullness of their lives.

The lyrics also see her encourage listeners to drop it like a "thot." "Thot" in African American English means "that hoe over there" and is often used in an insulting way to describe a girl who is perceived as promiscuous. A refrain also repeats the phrase "you bad." This is a clever and subversive way of reclaiming insults often leveled against women who do embrace their sexuality. In the song Beyoncé speaks to her friend and states that she's doing God's work by "going in." She is saying that her friend is doing God's work by living her life as her authentic self. Far from these messages of personal autonomy clashing with the Christian faith, much like the gospel and bounce in "CHURCH GIRL they exist in perfect harmony. The song talks about enjoyment, having fun, throwing ass, swimming through the oceans of cried tears. More importantly, it invites listeners to not accept judgment about any of these actions. The song holds space for the duality of these experiences and invites us to search for freedom rather than unattainable perfection and external validation.

With "CHURCH GIRL," Beyoncé also speaks of the beauty of independence. The lyrics to "CHURCH GIRL" describe Beyoncé as being happy on her own, without a man. These lyrics are also rebellious because conversative or traditional churches often prioritize heterosexual romantic love and marriage. This song and the *RENAISSANCE* album more broadly are about nontraditional community. Many people who have been shunned by some Christian communities, single women and queer folks included, have had to find their own chosen families, and the song's themes about bodily autonomy and not being judged for your sex life extend to both these communities. Beyoncé uses the song "CHURCH GIRL" to highlight the beauty of independence, friendships, and communities found outside of heterosexual romantic love.

A line from British Somali poet Warsan Shire that Beyoncé reads during *Lemonade* sees her describing pages from the Bible to stop the blood flow of her period, after she bathes in bleach. The line sees Shire describe the Bible as symbolic of the apparent need to cleanse herself of her womanhood. There is much to unpack within this line, but I find that it speaks to how Christianity can interact with or police femininity, and Scripture has been used to call what is natural "unclean." However, we must all find our identity outside of who we are on a Sunday morning *and* Saturday night. We must all stop calling ourselves unclean. For too long a place that should be all light—a church—has forced women to look inside themselves and only see darkness, punishing us for our God-given humanity. This song is an anthem for anyone who has ever dealt with shame, for anyone whose hips or lips have even been too "loose," and for those who have found judgment in a place where only freedom should reside.

We must all reject purity culture and embrace the rich tapestry of Black womanhood, and playing "CHURCH GIRL" and throwing it back with your hands on the nearest chair is a wonderful place to start. Ultimately, bodily autonomy does not exist in opposition to Christianity—far from it. Our bodies are ours, and joy is our divine right. We as humans blur the lines between the sacred and the scandalous, the holy and the carnal. This beautiful duality is represented in the mix of gospel and bounce in "CHURCH GIRL" as well as in the explicit lyrics that sound like worship. This duality is liberating as Beyoncé acknowledges the strange dichotomy of subservience and independence in the modern-day church girl. She embraces the full spectrum of what a church girl can be. In exploring how her Christian upbringing and faith can coexist beautifully with her identity as an independent and sexually liberated woman, she encourages us all to embrace our own supposed contradictions. As with her previous exploration of anger and tenderness in *Lemonade*, her exploration of her own duality in "CHURCH GIRL" shows that who she is as a person does not exist at the expense of who she is as an artist.

However, Beyoncé explores how healing can also be found outside of traditional Christianity. The African spiritual symbolism in *Lemonade* and later in *BLACK IS KING* serves as a backdrop for healing as well as personal introspection and cultural reclamation. These two albums see her reference cultural and religious practices from across the African continent as well as from Cuba and the American South. These references and ideas are found in the practice of voodoo, a religion practiced in parts of the Caribbean (especially Haiti) and in some Southern states.[3] It can combine elements of Roman Catholic ritual with traditional African magical and religious traditions, ones that are frequently characterized by sorcery and spirit possession. While voodoo was practiced by free and enslaved Black people, it particularly thrived within the Creole culture of the Louisiana Territory. White slave holders were scared, and they regarded voodoo as an evil practice, dark magic by a dark and savage people. After all, it is so easy to misinterpret the unknown and magical. These beliefs have become internalized to some, and many people from many communities have internalized the fear of practices such as tarot and healing crystals. By reclaiming these images Beyoncé makes the point that this type of faith and spirituality is as much a part of her heritage as Christianity and the Black Church. In the visuals and lyrics for both albums we see these time-old symbols that Black women have used to heal, stretching across West Africa, the Louisiana Bayou, and the Caribbean.[4]

The most prominent example of these diasporic images is the previously mentioned image of the Yoruba goddess Oshun in *Lemonade* and Beyoncé's 2017 Grammy performance. We know that Beyoncé uses Oshun imagery to connect to the divine feminine and her power as a woman, which is very much in keeping with the theme of *Lemonade*. However, these images also connect her and this body of work to a type of spirituality that is often demonized and misunderstood. The *Lemonade* visuals see Black women paint themselves, dive off buildings into water without drowning, and command fire and water with equal majesty. Later these women also dance on water in long white dresses and with an ease of movement that suggests they are, in fact, walking on it. Behind these stunning visuals is a reminder that there is power in these ancient traditions and that witches are just what men call powerful women. She shows us, musically and visually, the beauty in both the goddess and the witch, and how Black women have found healing in all these spiritual practices as well as in the church.

In *Lemonade*, Beyoncé explores how Black women have always been alchemists and how Black girl magic is much deeper than a slogan or hashtag—it is a fact. The dancers have intricately painted art on their face and body, highlighting their beauty rather than concealing it. This art derives from a spiritual ritual in worship of Orishas, the gods in the Yoruba religion. Inscribing who you are on your face with markings or scars or paint is common throughout the wider African diaspora in places such as Cuba and Louisiana. It is notable that Beyoncé has chosen practices that link the diaspora and have strong links to Southern America. The point is clear. There is nothing to fear here in this so-called voodoo. These references represent Beyoncé embracing the divine feminine and reconnecting with an aspect of spirituality and faith taken from Black American women. In *Lemonade* and *RENAISSANCE*, Beyoncé calls on her ancestors more than once. The lyrics tether Beyoncé to the women who have come before her as she harnesses their power and wisdom. By engaging in these ancient spiritual customs Beyoncé furthers the central argument of her recent bodies of work—Black womanhood is sacred—and the strength Black women have had to harness to survive is shared.

BLACK IS KING saw Beyoncé engage with these themes even further. She talks about charging her crystals in a full moon in "BLACK PARADE." It is important that she references spiritual practices originating in African countries in a song in which she exclaims her pride in her Blackness. The full moon is a very important symbol in these spiritual practices and beliefs, often linked to divine feminine energy. The moon is also said to act as a cleansing and energizing force, both for people and for crystals. She compares her little sister to Yemaya, the mother of all Orishas and humanity. By weaving these references into the art for *BLACK IS KING*, Beyoncé illustrates that being proud of her Blackness involves reclaiming these traditions, beliefs, and remedies that white supremacy has robbed Black women of. I believe that witchcraft is just a shorthand to describe anything powerful women are accused of, and the negative perceptions of traditional spiritual practices are rooted in racism as well as sexism. Similarly, the fear of voodoo is nothing but a fear of, and lack of information about, ancient African spirituality.

During the refrain in "CHURCH GIRL," Beyoncé promises to keeping loving herself, which really is the message of the song. Her work has so often combined love and reverence for spiritual practices as well as an appreciation for her upbringing in the Southern Black Church; she sees beauty in it all. Faith is a complicated thing, and no one has had to have more faith and belief in themselves than Black women. I firmly believe that any faith or religion should start from a place of acceptance, not shame. Ultimately, it is this acceptance that I hear in Beyoncé's music. We all need release from the shackles and expectations others have for us. I exist like we all do in blurred boundaries, and the parts of me that should clash in fact make the most wonderful song to dance to in whichever way I choose. No pastor, partner, or white supremacist structure should control your body and how you choose to move it. While we must allow space for who we are on a Sunday afternoon and a Saturday evening, we must not allow any space for shame.

BLACK MOTHERHOOD AS PERFORMANCE AND POLITICS

Beyoncé is many things, including a mother, and throughout her career she has redefined what it means to be a Black mother in public. Unlike traditional celebrity motherhood (which often appears passive or image-based), she engages with themes of motherhood in her work. Health complications and challenges mean that I (like so many) have a complicated relationship with motherhood. However, the way Beyoncé represents motherhood and legacy still makes me feel seen and heard. From songs for her children, to the theme of ancestorial inheritance in her later projects, she constructs motherhood as part of her mythos—visual, musical, and undeniably divine.

Her pregnancy announcement at the 2011 MTV Video Music Awards was both hypervisible and yet controlled. She sung "Love on Top" (with choreography and every single key change no less) before opening her bright pink sparkly blazer to reveal a baby bump that would soon become Blue Ivy Carter. Everyone in the room celebrated the moment, including Jay-Z, who the camera then panned to as he hugged his friends. The announcement also generated a high response online at a time in which viral moments were slowly becoming a thing. Why this moment spoke to so many was because this was more than simply celebrity culture; it was celebration for a Black maternal body in a space that rarely celebrates it.

Later, she also announced her pregnancy with twins Sir and Rumi in a typically artistic way, this time with a photoshoot. The 2017 maternity photos, a collaboration with artist Awol Erizku, are abundant with references to Renaissance depictions of the Madonna and Child motif and Venus, as well as to Yoruban deities such as Oshun, who Beyoncé often references in her work. With these historical references, the photos are still in keeping with current internet aesthetics and trends relevant today. These photos show Beyoncé as a religious icon meets digital-age fertility goddess within a Botticelli-inspired photoshoot. Also, who can forget her 2017 Grammy performance while heavily pregnant with her twins, a performance that was introduced by her own mother, Tina Knowles, who stated that she had "a mother's pride."[1] Beyoncé took to the stage in a gorgeous jewel-encrusted gown and gold headpiece, fit for a queen.

The performance was a stunning ode to mothers and women featuring a medley of her *Lemonade* songs including the emotional "Sandcastles" and "Love Drought" along with the poetry by Warsan Shire featured on the album. The nine-minute performance featured countless women, as well as a stunt involving a leaning chair, which raised all our blood pressures. Beyoncé mixed traditional Christian iconography of the Virgin Mary with references to Orishas and other diasporic images. In one moment, her dancers became disciples in a nod to the iconic *The Last Supper* painting by Leonardo da Vinci. Not many could pull off referencing *The Last Supper* and Oshun in the same performance, but Beyoncé did. She used different faiths to explore the universal beauty and strength of motherhood. These images she referenced in her performance may differ drastically in origins, but they do not clash—they exist in harmony and beauty because there is not a singular way to practice faith, or to be a church girl, or to connect with our spirituality and motherhood.

This performance grows in significance when we consider what we know about her complicated journey to motherhood. While she is usually a private person, Beyoncé has shared some details about giving birth, especially her trying to get pregnant the first time and the complicated birth with her twins. In the 2018 September issue of *Vogue*, she stated "After the C-section, my core felt different. It had been major surgery. Some of your organs are shifted temporarily, and in rare cases, removed temporarily during delivery."[2] She is not alone in having a complicated birth, especially among fellow Black women, and sharing these details illuminated the story of those women as well as her own. The Centers for Disease Control and Prevention reports that Black women have a three to four times higher risk of pregnancy-related death than white women in America, with many of these deaths being linked to medical negligence as well as conditions such as preeclampsia. Serena Williams, who would later star in *Lemonade* alongside Beyoncé, also gave birth via emergency C-section and had potentially life-threatening complications after. Seeing the biggest stars in the world deal with maternal health problems and health care racism was simultaneously validating and scary for so many of us.[3]

Despite these harsh realities and the challenges Beyoncé faced during both of her pregnancies, which she shared so much of with the world, she was still subjected to awful and harmful rumors that she was in fact not pregnant with Blue Ivy and instead used a surrogate. While rumors about celebrities are common, when you consider the trauma that she had to endure while giving birth, this conversation felt so violent. Because she headlined the Glastonbury Festival while pregnant, many believed this was an impossible feat. We watched her maintain the high standard she set for herself and her career, as mothers do every day. However, there were those who would not believe she could perform the way she did while pregnant. The odd fascination with her first pregnancy went beyond normal celebrity gossip and seemed to be a way of diminishing the power of Black women and what Beyoncé had achieved while being pregnant. Many of us who have been following Beyoncé's career believe this rumor and period caused a shift in how she approaches the public. Following the birth of Blue Ivy, Beyoncé began to be even more private and engage with the public in a more controlled and specific manner.

If we explore how Beyoncé presents motherhood, we can begin to understand how her presentation of Black motherhood is politicized. Images of Black motherhood and domesticity are a specific point of interest and contention, dating back to the time of slavery. Since then, as sociologists have noted, "the Black female body marked by society and its conceptions of what it is and embodies, continues to operate within the hegemonic order that defines America."[4] Many sociologists and historians, including bell hooks in her book *Reel to Real: Race, Class and Sex at the Movies*, have argued that portrayals of Black mothers in popular culture often reenforced negative stereotypes about Black women and reduced them to simply "caregivers."[5] A popular stereotype of Black motherhood is represented by "the mammy." Historically, the mammy depicts Black women as domestic workers, specifically caring for children in white homes. The stereotype originated during slavery but was also heavily referenced during the Jim Crow era and in American popular culture since then. It is this context, alongside the Black maternal health crisis, that makes images of Black motherhood so important.

In defiance of the forces that seek to define Black women by their role as caregivers, Beyoncé has openly balanced her career alongside her journey to motherhood. As a fan, I see her maintain her career while raising her family and feel this has been truly something to behold. She has documented training and performing at the Glastonbury Festival while pregnant, as well as her intense preparation after she gave birth for her Coachella headline set. Her *Homecoming* documentary highlighted the toll of post-partum performance. She stated, "I was a woman that had just given birth to twins, and I insisted on doing Coachella." During the documentary we see her finish a long day of rehearsals and then joke about having to get to her "fifty-leven children."[6] A mother's work is truly never done, even when that work is on one of the biggest stages of the world. Due to the control so many people feel over Black women's bodies, our motherhood is politicized, but Beyoncé showcased the beauty in family life while not being defined by her family life, which is a public rejection of these historic stereotypes. Black women can be mothers and caregivers without being reduced to these roles at the expense of their career and other aspects of their life and womanhood. Of course, these facts are larger than Beyoncé, but seeing her at this stage of her life, as she maintains her agency, creativity, and talent, is validating and informative for many.

Much of Beyoncé's work after she gave birth sees her use music as a personal maternal archive. For instance, "Blue" from her self-titled album and "BROWN SKIN GIRL" from *The Lion King: The Gift*, both featuring Blue Ivy, act as sonic expressions of mothering. These songs see Beyoncé hand down advice and confidence through music that archives, protects, and nurtures. In "Blue" Beyoncé sings about how her children and family allow her to find solace from her hectic lifestyle. During the outro we even hear Blue Ivy call to her mother, whose name she adorably pronounces as "Bee-sy."[7] "BROWN SKIN GIRL" tackles how to raise a daughter who loves herself in a world that does not, another act of mothering through music. Blue Ivy's feature on "BROWN SKIN GIRL" earned the BET Her award, and thus she became the youngest BET award winner in history. The video also won Best Music Video at the 63rd Annual Grammy Awards, making Blue Ivy the youngest individually credited Grammy recipient. In the video and in these samples, Blue Ivy is more than simply Beyoncé's, or "Bee-sy's," child—she is Black girl joy personified.

Years after she featured on "Blue" and "BROWN SKIN GIRL," Blue Ivy joined her mom on tour for *RENAISSANCE*, taking to the stage to dance for three songs. What was initially meant to be a one-off event became a much-loved part of the tour with Blue Ivy gracing stages across the world. Blue Ivy in popular imagination has become more than just Beyoncé's child—she's an inheritor of cultural capital, an artist, and a continuation of the matriarchal project. Beyoncé's children have continued to influence her art with the *BLACK IS KING* project being dedicated to Sir Carter and two songs on *COWBOY CARTER* being dedicated to and featuring Rumi. *COWBOY CARTER*'s "PROTECTOR" provides a beautiful insight on motherhood, with Beyoncé claiming that although her children can shine on their own, she is there to project their light, so it shines even brighter.

Beyoncé also frequently centers her own mother (Tina Knowles) in her music. In doing so she places herself within a lineage of Black Southern women who survived—and thrived—despite living under patriarchy and white supremacy. In "LEVII'S JEANS," a love song on *COWBOY CARTER*, she says that she "got it" from her mother, a point she also makes on the remix of "Savage" by fellow Houston icon Megan Thee Stallion. While these may be humorous lyrics displaying her well-placed confidence in her body and physical appearance, she also uses her music to describe the deeper and more valuable things she has inherited from her mother. Visuals from *Lemonade* and *BLACK IS KING* illustrate Beyoncé becoming part of a longer matrilineal chain. On *Lemonade*, the spoken-word poetry talks directly about ancestral women and how the protagonist resembles her mother but is also completely different from the women in her lineage. Her lyrics and art frame mothering as not only a biological act, but an ancestral and spiritual journey.

Motherhood is power, and that is apparent from the personal journey Beyoncé has chosen to share with us while being at the top of her game. In her discography, Beyoncé continuously demonstrates how mothering is not only something biological; it is an action that can also extend beyond a woman's immediate family. In *RENAISSANCE* and on the RENAISSANCE World Tour, she becomes "mother of the house Renaissance." Rather than being a literal or biological mother, she becomes a mother to the queer people who need chosen family. This references the legendary drag mothers who would look after young queer people in the ball scene who are in need of safety and guidance. This mothering was evident when she expressed gratitude and pride for the "safe space" she was able to create for her fans. Throughout her other bodies of work Beyoncé invokes Oshun (in *Lemonade*), the Earth Mother (for her maternity shoot with the twins), and cosmic feminine archetypes such as the Black Madonna across her career. Her examination of motherhood isn't just personal; it's mythic and symbolic. She embodies *mother* not just as something she is but as symbol of Black continuity and creativity. I personally don't know what it means to be a mother, though I question whether any of us do really. It's a job there is no training for. But I do know that mothering creates a legacy, whether emotional or physical. I also know that to embrace motherhood as a Black woman is to nurture in a world and society that has often not nurtured you, and that is a radical act.

BEYONCÉ, FOOTBALL, A CHRISTMAS FUNERAL, MY GRANDMA, AND LEGACY

Christmas and the weeks around it can be a complicated time. They bring conversations that are usually avoided, arguments, and for me, often a feeling of alienation. There are the usual complicated family dynamics, some specific to me being mixed-race with white family members, but Christmas remains a time where I think about my grandma. Her birthday was on the fourteenth of December, and as she and my granddad were devout Christians, they naturally adored Christmas. She died when I had just finished university, and I hope that she is proud of who I have become. Hers was a heavily attended funeral; people had to stand, while others reserved spaces next to them on the pews like her funeral was some kind of concert. Despite being busy, the funeral still felt so intimate, and I think that's because of how she made everyone feel like close family. I have trouble recalling the specific details of that day, what Bible passages were read and what the weather was, but I have a vivid recollection of being overwhelmed by the amount of love and laughter there was in that church and in her favorite hotel for the service after. Most of all, I remember the laughs I shared with my cousins. These laughs were not sad because of our shared loss; rather these moments were perfectly timed and completely appropriate. I can still picture her four daughters carrying her coffin. My grandma was a rebellious soul. She would encourage me to dye my hair pink or purple, then inform my grandad that she was going to copy me. Our family dinners always involved her telling us some ridiculous but undeniably true story about her youth and the businesses she used to run. On one car ride she borrowed my large and bright pink sunglasses because she "wanted to look like a poet." Ultimately, she embraced the Christian traditions of loving everyone and consuming wine. I'm not sure if it's because of the Christmases we shared or her birthday or the wine we drank, but naturally I think about her at Christmas.

On Christmas Day 2024, Beyoncé performed a thirteen-minute concert streamed on Netflix called *A Cowboy Carter Christmas*. This was during the halftime show for the NFL game between the Houston Texans and the Baltimore Ravens, a performance now known as Beyoncé Bowl. What was interesting to me about Beyoncé Bowl is that it was hosted in Houston, Beyoncé's hometown and the perfect place to perform songs from her *COWBOY CARTER* album. The first song on *COWBOY CARTER* is called "AMERIICAN REQUIEM," a requiem of course being a mass or musical celebration for a dead person. It's a beautiful song that explores the bittersweet nature of endings. Notably, she did not perform "AMERIICAN REQUIEM" during Beyoncé Bowl. However, while the song was absent from the set list it soon became clear to me that with this performance Beyoncé was giving us an American requiem for her fictional cowboy alter ego, Cowboy Carter. The show begins with her emerging from a bright light and ends with a gunshot as she is suspended on a platform over the field. Some may argue that Christmas isn't a good time to talk about death, but I'd argue the opposite. I believe there is no better time for reflection. There is no better time to honor the dead, with wine of course.

The first visual of Beyoncé Bowl was Beyoncé riding on a tall, seemingly white horse. Her characteristic blonde curls framed her face, and she wore a large white cowboy hat with a white fur coat. In "BLACK PARADE," from *The Lion King: The Gift*, Beyoncé mentions wearing tight white clothes to a funeral. This is in reference to the African American tradition of wearing white clothes in honor of someone's passing. This tradition was on firm display during her Beyoncé Bowl performance, this American requiem. Beyoncé, the dancers, and her fellow artists were dressed in all white apart from a sprinkling of denim jeans and a Black woman and Black man draped in the American flag while standing on top of a horse. As the story of the performance became clear, I realized that they were wearing all "tight white" to a funeral. Aside from the overall story of the performance, she used this opportunity to shine a light on Black culture in front of her twenty-four million viewers. They were at a funeral, but they were also going to party and provide a history lesson at the same time. In "AMERIICAN REQUIEM" Beyoncé asks listeners to truly consider the argument that her music is not country: If her music doesn't qualify as country, then what does? With this line the argument and thesis of *COWBOY CARTER* asserts that if we're going out, we're going out with what's ours.

Funerals, wakes, and requiems are the perfect place to honor the culture and traditions of the departed. During this requiem that twenty-four million people attended from various bedrooms, living rooms, and countries, Beyoncé provided a lesson on Black Southern culture and the history of Black cowboys. One that was seamlessly incorporated into the performance was a floral carriage, which she included to reference the early Juneteenth parades held in Emancipation Park in Houston, Texas. Emancipation Park is Houston's oldest public park and has held Juneteenth celebrations for well over 150 years. Not only are these events a chance to celebrate and reflect, but the residents also utilize the opportunity to champion local businesses and Black impact on the area. This grows even further in significance as Emancipation Park was founded on June 19, 1872, specifically to commemorate the end of slavery by four previously enslaved men.[1] Every year since then Juneteenth has been celebrated to honor the enslaved people in Texas. Juneteenth is of special significance to the African American community in Texas as Texan enslaved people were the last to find out that they were free as it took the US army months to enforce the Emancipation Proclamation due to the strong Confederate control in that location. The Union troops arrived in Galveston Bay on June 19, 1865. Beyoncé used the performance to shine a light on the historic Emancipation Park celebrations and the community they honor.

Beyoncé was joined by a group known as the Compton Cowboys, who also produced a part of the show. They are based in the inner-city area of Compton in Los Angeles, known for fostering talent such as Kendrick Lamar and Serena Williams. They use horseback riding and equestrian culture to provide a positive influence for inner-city youth, mostly young Black men. They also compete and aim to break into the rodeo circuit, bringing Black representation to a predominately white sport. In a moment that was crucial to those like me who were completely emerged in the world of popular culture, actor Alex Fine joined the performance as part of the Compton Cowboys. Alex Fine, husband to singer Cassie Ventura, has been very critical of abuse in the music industry and of Diddy specifically. Nothing Beyoncé does is unintentional. The Compton Cowboys' slogan is "the streets raised us; horses saved us."[2] To understand their mission, and this performance, you must understand the link between African Americans and cowboy culture. Cowboy culture and horses in general are seen as belonging to a white wealthy sport culture like equestrianism despite the long history of Black cowboys. Historians estimate that post–Civil War, one in four cowboys were Black.[3] Black cowboys and cattle farmers have long been a backbone of Southern culture. In fact, African American scholar William Loren Katz argues that "after the Civil War, being a cowboy was one of the few jobs open to men of color."[4] Despite their contributions and skill, African American cowboys faced discrimination in the very towns in which they worked. However, they found safety and solace within their communities. Even when opportunities for working cowboys were on the decline due to the shifting economy, the public's fascination with the cowboy lifestyle prevailed. This fascination made way for the popularity of Wild West stories, rodeos, and the modern rodeo circuit. Bill Pickett, born in 1870 in Texas to formerly enslaved parents, became one of the most famous early rodeo stars. In 1972, forty years after his death, Pickett became the first Black honoree in the National Rodeo Hall of Fame, and rodeo athletes still honor his legacy by competing at the Bill Pickett Invitational Rodeo today.[5]

Beyoncé opened the Beyoncé Bowl singing "16 CARRIAGES." Just to give us a second to reflect on this, she sung the show-stopping country-as-hell ballad "16 CARRIAGES" while riding a horse—look at the breath control. As Beyoncé disembarked from the horse, the camera panned to Black people standing around, and on, white horses. Alongside these ethereal and beautiful Black people were the Black woman and Black man draped in the American flag, some of the only color we see in the entire thirteen minutes of her performance, a visual representation of making our own American dream. A few of the dancers standing on horses demonstrated the Black tradition of "trick riding."[6] Also, from what I can tell, the specific horses used were Lipizzaner horses. Aside from being elegant and smart horses, this breed has a dark coat that turns whiteish gray with age.[7] In a show about country music this metaphor is perfect as the Black influence on country music has been gradually stripped from the genre to the point where now it may look white, but it never was.

Beyoncé then transitioned to a performance of her soulful and understated version of "BLACKBIIRD" with the featured country singers from the track: Tanner Adell, Brittney Spencer, Tiera Kennedy, and Reyna Roberts. Four Black women of different skin tones and sizes dressed in flowing white dresses is a sight that completely fits within what Beyoncé has been increasingly doing with her discography, but something about the beauty of this image still took me by surprise. This "BLACKBIIRD" performance saw her bring other Black women in country music into the limelight and onto the world stage. After this song Beyoncé then walked through a bright white light onto the football field.

If the whole performance was a requiem, then it was also a perfect celebration of life and love. In death I think we would all like to be remembered for how we lived and loved, and as much as the performance may have been the story of a death, it was also about love and joy. After she walked into the light following the haunting version of "BLACKBIIRD," she launched into "YA YA," one of the most upbeat songs on the album and a personal favorite of mine. She introduced "YA YA" by counting down from three, or in her case, "tre." Tre is the loving nickname for the Third Ward of Houston where Beyoncé is from. She was then joined by the Ocean of Soul Marching Band from Texas Southern University, a historically Black college. In fact, Texas Southern University is one of the largest HBCUs in the country. This performance felt reminiscent of *Homecoming*, not only because of the all-encompassing nature of a Beyoncé performance, but because of the light shone on Black culture and HBCUs. As "YA YA" states, history *cannot* be erased.

Beyoncé then transitioned to "MY HOUSE," a song released as part of *Renaissance: A Film by Beyoncé*. In "MY HOUSE" Beyoncé asks listeners to shout the name of the person they came to see, then answers her own question with "me." This was a nod to those of us who were not in that stadium for the football. Performing "MY HOUSE" also linked this *COWBOY CARTER* second-act performance to the first act, *RENAISSANCE*, intentionally continuing the story of this trilogy that will presumably end with the yet unreleased act 3.

Beyoncé performed "SWEET ★ HONEY ★ BUCKIIN'," another personal highlight for me from *COWBOY CARTER* that features country singer and rapper Shaboozey. Shaboozey is a

Nigerian Virginian Black country singer with locs who has been dominating the charts in recent years following his features on *COWBOY CARTER*, especially with his 2024 song "A Bar Song (Tipsy.)" As much as Shaboozey is making waves (or locs) within the genre, he has also been rejected by it, and like Beyoncé he has also been alienated by the Country Music Awards specifically. *Rolling Stone* magazine argued that Shaboozey deserves an apology from the 2024 Country Music Awards.[8] As well as not receiving either of the two awards he was nominated for, he was subjected to microaggressions from winning acts during the award ceremony about the pronunciation of his name. As he and Beyoncé have both been somewhat rejected by the country music establishment, he has supported Beyoncé and vice versa. For this performance he wore a stunning long white coat and mandatory cowboy hat. During his verse he raps that he does not care about how other people categorize his music, he's proud of his country roots, and, like Beyoncé, he wants to reclaim this whitewashed genre. Beyoncé walks off camera while saluting him to give him his moment. The camera then pans back to reveal Beyoncé as she launches into what I believe to be some of her best choreography to date. There is no good funeral or life without love, and to bring the romance part of the story to the stage she then moves to "LEVII'S JEANS" with Post Malone. As well as being a country love song, this is a song about partnership and is arguably the most romantic song on *COWBOY CARTER*. "LEVII'S JEANS" is then followed by Beyoncé's version of "Jolene." A song made popular by country icon Dolly Parton, Beyoncé's "JOLENE" speaks to the pain of love and jealousy that are a part of life. As mentioned, this performance may have been a requiem, but before the metaphorical death of this alter ego, love, jealousy, and all the other emotions must be experienced.

The climax of the show is her performance of "TEXAS HOLD 'EM." It was only right for her to perform the chart-topping song live for the first time in Texas. This performance of a country song in Houston was certainly a full circle moment for her career from where she started with Girl's Tyme in the Third Ward. Blue Ivy also graced the stage, adding to the gravity of the moment. Only a week prior to the performance, Blue Ivy attended a film premiere and was met with criticism that her dress was inappropriate because it showed her bare arms. For the Beyoncé Bowl, Blue Ivy danced in a fitted bright white outfit next to her mother. Her arms and long braids were on full display, unapologetically. I don't know whether it was the fact that Beyoncé brought Blue Ivy on stage or because it was Christmas and so I was already thinking of my grandma, but I started thinking about legacy. I thought of motherhood, of my mother carrying my grandma's coffin, of the times my mother and grandmother danced next to each other, of the times I've danced with my mom, how our mothers can be the source of our shame but also the antidote to it. If a requiem should prompt us to think about anything, I guess it should be our legacy. Watching this thirteen-minute performance about life and death and everything in between prompted me to vow that my legacy will not include shame. Instead, it will absolutely include dancing.

As I write this, I don't know what the legacy of this Beyoncé Bowl performance will be. Maybe Netflix will continue with live streamed performances and football games; maybe Beyoncé Bowl will be removed from viewing and the Beyhive will storm the Netflix offices with placards. I don't know where this requiem will end up, but I know that I spent Christmas 2024 completely immersed in the story of *COWBOY CARTER* and in awe of the rich culture of the Black American South. In "SPAGHETTII" Beyoncé exclaims that she is not a "regular" singer. She invites listeners confidently to come and get what they are owed, and on Christmas Day 2024 we did just that. Twenty-four million US viewers and Netflix subscribers in over two hundred countries tuned in to the Beyoncé Bowl, aka some football game.[9] As we saw with *Homecoming* and her Super Bowl performances, there is something all-encompassing about her presence, and on Christmas Day 2024 she filled the football field and our homes with talent and history.

Those who say Beyoncé is overrated are perhaps neglecting how many cultural references and the level of talent she can bring to a thirteen-minute performance. Whether it was the flower carriages honoring Juneteenth in Texas, or the Black men riding horses and displaying their tricks while draped in the American flag, *A Cowboy Carter Christmas* was, as so much of her music is, bigger than Beyoncé. Everything about the show was intentional, from the religious symbolism, to the specific camera angles taking us on a journey around an entire football field (which I'm told is quite big). As a historian I find these references to historical and cultural moments to be infinitely fascinating. But what is more important to me about the performance is what it gave me on that Christmas Day. It gave me praise, joy, and permission to reclaim anything that is ever taken from me. It also gave me one of the most beautiful portrayals of death that I have ever seen. *COWBOY CARTER* as an album is cyclical. It ends with a song called "AMEN," as any good church service or funeral does. "AMEN" samples the first song on the album, "AMERIICAN REQUIEM." This endless loop pays homage to the circle of life. While watching the performance, I hoped that at my requiem there is half as much love and joy as I found during Beyoncé Bowl and at my grandma's favorite hotel following her funeral. The best requiems honor the spirt of those we have lost, the final moment to teach us something about their life, and *A Cowboy Carter Christmas* was no exception. If *RENAISSANCE* is about joy as revolution, then *COWBOY CARTER* and this performance is about legacy and holding on to what is ours till the day that we die.

ACT IV

ENCORE—
WHY BEYONCÉ'S MUSIC AND PERFORMANCES STAY WITH US

"THE MIC IS ON"—THE POWER AND ELEVATION OF BEYONCÉ'S LIVE PERFORMANCES

In April 2024 *Rolling Stone* magazine named Beyoncé the greatest living entertainer.[1] This is a well-deserved accolade not only due to her vocal ability on her discography and in the consistently stunning videos that accompany them, but in large part because of how show-stopping and life-altering her performances are. As my personal experience can attest, not much can compare to seeing Beyoncé live. After attending a show, I have found it hard to describe a Beyoncé performance to those who haven't had the privilege. Everything from the lighting to the story the show tells is intentional and highlights how a Beyoncé live show is so much more than a performance. The talent of her singing and dancing is always catapulted to a new level with innovative stage designs and the talent she surrounds herself with on stage. Luvvie Ajayi, a writer and fellow member of the Hive, points out that Beyoncé shows up for every show as if it is her last, as if she still needs to impress us.[2] Nothing compares to seeing Beyoncé live because of the combination of her talent with her attention to detail, and to paraphrase Luvvie Ajayi—we are always impressed.

Witnessing Beyoncé perform can often change how you respond to her albums. For example, it was clear from its release that *RENAISSANCE* was a party album, but seeing the songs from it performed live, with the onstage ball culture and dancers, expanded the album and put us all inside the music. She utilizes the stage and visual mediums to contribute to the meaning of her art. For a start, Beyoncé surrounds herself with excellence. Whether it's an HBCU marching band or queer dancers who can turn a football-stadium stage into an intimate ball, if you're on stage with Beyoncé, then you must embody brilliance simply to keep up. Even those who might not consider themselves fans have to acknowledge the skill in her live performances. For these reasons, if we are to call Beyoncé the greatest living entertainer, her live performances are perhaps the most compelling argument for this accolade.

Beyoncé has always prioritized giving amazing and standout performances. She's a perfectionist, approaching her live shows with characteristic Virgo attention to detail. It is impossible to compete with her showmanship, even if her performance includes just her and a mic. In 2006 Beyoncé sung "Listen" on *The Oprah Winfrey Show*. She stood in a beautiful gown and red lip, letting her vocal performance steal the show.[3] Even during these stripped-back performances, there is such depth and talent where she lets her voice carry the show. She does not need a stadium and ten costume changes to connect with an audience, as we have seen time and time again; she can command a room just with her voice alone. Performances that highlight her ability to maintain vocal control while dancing intense choreography are as impressive as her simply singing with a mic and a ball gown in front of President Obama.

Even early in her career Beyoncé's live performances were in a league of their own. Her first performance as a solo artist was at the 2003 Essence Awards where she performed her number one single, "Crazy in Love." Following the Essence Awards, she also took to the stage at the 2003 BET Awards to perform "Crazy in Love" in front of a giant sign of her name. These early performances had the confident choreography we would come to expect with her powerhouse vocals and had her former girl-group members cheering her on in the audience. Of all the Beyoncé shows I have missed, either because I was ten, or in the wrong country, or didn't have the money to buy a ticket, these 2003 Essence and BET performances are the ones I would have most enjoyed. I think it was clear from these early performances, even though they are a far cry from the show-stopping events she now does, that live performances would become integral to Beyoncé's creative output. She has always treated performance as its own medium to excel in and not just an extension of her albums or singles.

A year after the BET and Essence performances and still relatively early on in her solo career, Beyoncé more than kept up with the musical legend that is Prince when she joined him on stage at the 2004 Grammys. She and Prince performed a string of his hits, later transitioning into a chorus of her hit "Crazy in Love," while he accompanied her on guitar with a stunning and unforgettable showmanship one can always expect from Prince. As Beyoncé was a young artist at the time, receiving Prince's seal of approval was an accomplishment. Another example of an early performance that would prove to be an indicator of what was to come was "Ring the Alarm" at the 2006 MTV Video Music Awards. To start, she dropped from the ceiling on a rope in a floor-length trench coat and heels with a gorgeous two-piece underneath.[4] When I think about Beyoncé embracing feminine rage, this performance of this hell-hath-no-fury anthem springs to mind. The sharp choreography and production gave us a taste of how Beyoncé would continue to dominate stages.

From a two-piece under a trench coat, to haute couture, a Beyoncé show will never neglect the fashion. Far from being just a costume, Beyoncé uses fashion as a storytelling medium to further the meaning of the music. As mentioned, during the RENAISSANCE World Tour, fashion became even more integral to the show. Her stage looks often involve a body suit and/or shorts, and it *always* sparkles. When I look at these performances, with their intense choreography and vocals, it is hard to imagine that she would be able to elevate them even further as she grew and developed as an artist.

Alongside her musical developments, Beyoncé transitioned from the classic expectations of live performances toward creating artistic experiences on stage. One such masterpiece came with her I Am... Tour. The tour ran from 2009 to 2010 to support her 2008 album *I Am... Sasha Fierce*. It was a theatrical tour with two stages and a ten-piece all-female band. If you compare the performances of "Crazy in Love" during this tour to her earlier performances of the song, it is apparent that even in this short time, her stagecraft had elevated. She captivated audiences by switching between her alter ego, Sasha Fierce, and herself, something she established with the album. When she channels Sasha Fierce, Beyoncé is more confident and sensual, the more daring dance moves and skintight leotards reflecting Sasha's fearlessness. During the ballads she would switch to her own identity, wearing flowing white, and give stunning renditions of the less confident but more honest moments from the album. For me, this album and tour tried to answer the difficult question of who we are we when no one is watching. Where does *I Am*...end and *Sasha Fierce* begin? This tour was particularly validating because after all aren't we endlessly caught between other people's perceptions of us and the truth?

The year 2009 saw the inauguration of President Obama, the first Black president of the United States. Beyoncé performed a rendition of Etta James's "At Last" for the first dance at the inauguration. For President Obama's second inauguration, in 2013, she sang the national anthem. These were not sparkly performances with a team of dancers that one may expect at a Beyoncé show; rather they were stripped-back and vocally superb renditions of both songs. Infamously, the 2013 performance was subjected to accusations of lip-synching. While these suspicions did turn out to be true, Beyoncé still silenced critics by singing live at a Super Bowl press conference and informing journalists that she had lip-synched at the inauguration because there wasn't enough time for her to rehearse for the historic performance.[5] Even if you find representation politics lacking and unradical (a more-than-valid point of view), this performance was soulful and highlighted the optimism many felt about this new chapter in history. Demonstrating her range as an entertainer, a year later Beyoncé performed a mash-up of her song "If Were a Boy" and the alternative rock hit "You Oughta Know" by Alanis Morissette at the 2010 Grammy Awards.[6] This performance tackled two very different songs with similar themes. She belted out "If I Were a Boy" with head banging before going into the Alanis Morissette classic. Both songs explore themes of romantic disrespect, and these performances proved that all that Beyoncé needs to give a great performance is a microphone (but a fan and intense choreography never hurts).

The year 2011 was monumental for Beyoncé as a performer. In May of 2011, at the Billboard Awards, Beyoncé produced something special. Since she'd be receiving Billboard's Millennium Award, she debuted her performance of "Run the World (Girls)." She was joined by a virtual battalion that she seamlessly danced with, as well as one hundred backup dancers. Throughout the performance she ruled her own nation and later confessed that she had never worked on anything harder.[7] This was one of the first times we saw the full potential of what, and just how big, a Beyoncé production could be, potential that was fully realized when she headlined the Glastonbury Festival later that year.

On June 26, 2011, Beyoncé became the first woman in twenty years to headline the pyramid stage in Glastonbury. It may be hard to imagine today, but her place as the titular act at a traditionally rock and roll/alternative music festival was controversial.[8] For that year at least, the Glastonbury Festival swapped men with guitars for women in hot pants, and it was good. She sang a slew of hits including "Crazy in Love" (of course), some Destiny's Child classics, and her much beloved duet with Lady Gaga, "Telephone." While festivals are not equipped for the intricate stage design she often includes, she still dominated the unusually bare stage with vocals, choreography, and a wonderfully excessive amount of gold sequins. More importantly, she made people feel seen at a festival that doesn't usually cater to a hip-hop and R & B audience.[9]

The following August she performed "Love on Top" at the MTV VMAs in a sparkly blazer and wide-cut black trousers. When I listen to "Love on Top" I often count the key changes because it's such a vocally challenging song that requires quick transitions and almost superhuman breath control. She, of course, executed this song perfectly, alongside the coolest pregnancy reveal ever. In my opinion, of course. At the end of the song, she removed her earpiece, dropped her handheld mic, and revealed a baby bump that would soon become her "manager" and Grammy Award winner, Blue Ivy Carter. This was one of the earliest Beyoncé performances to "break the internet." Twitter's official global PR feed, Twitter Comms @TwitterGlobalPR, tweeted the following Monday that the baby news broke a site record at 10:35 p.m. EST, with 8,868 tweets per second, the most ever recorded for a single event.[10] Beyoncé can turn a stage into anything, including a pregnancy reveal.

While that was one of earliest Beyoncé moments to break my social media feed, it was far from the last. The Super Bowl halftime show is one of the most anticipated events of the pop culture calendar. Over the years, some of the biggest names in the music industry have taken to the stage to perform. In 2013, Beyoncé followed in the footsteps of Michael Jackson and Prince and headlined the Super Bowl XLVII halftime show in New Orleans on February 3.[11] Two logos of Beyoncé's profile were put on stage, and the show began with Beyoncé emerging from the floor between them while a blaze of flames appeared on stage. She performed a medley of her most iconic hits including "Crazy in Love," "Love on Top," "End of Time," and "Baby Boy." She gave us the mandatory "one hand on hip" strut to the intro of "Crazy in Love," and the performance was one of the most-tweeted-about moments of the time. Throughout the performance she was backed by her all-female band, her backup dancers, and the Saintsations, a thirty-two-girl cheerleader troupe for the New Orleans Saints. At the time it was the most watched Super Bowl halftime performance in history, with almost one-third of the population of the United States tuned in.[12] At this point in her career, her music was less overtly political; however, the performance did mark a turning point in the history of the Super Bowl halftime show. In the years since her performance, the iconic halftime show shifted from featuring primarily rock and pop bands to showcasing some of the biggest names in R & B and hip-hop; similar to her impact on the Glastonbury Festival, Beyoncé's notable performances often shift popular culture.

In 2014, Beyoncé received the Michael Jackson Video Vanguard Award at the MTV Video Music Awards.[13] At the ceremony she performed a medley of her songs. She drew on new chart-toppers as well as old classics to create a set that entertained and showcased her decades-long career. It was an undeniably sexy performance but performed with no men on stage and not catered to the male gaze. It was just her and her dancers, striking a dramatic pose—dressed as the world's most beautiful disco ball. This is also the time in her career when she began to be a bit more personal with her performances, with images of Blue Ivy and family vacations playing on-screen behind her while she sang "Blue." It was also in this performance that she stood with her hands on her hips in front of a sign declaring the word "Feminist." Her family, her feminism, and her talent were invited on the stage, and this would be far from the last time she placed her politics front and center. She performed "Pretty Hurts," "Haunted," and "No Angel," often giving us just snippets of these songs. To incorporate her vast discography, mash-ups and medleys have become a staple of Beyoncé's live performances. Fans often anticipate these mash-ups because she has turned them into a device to create yet more magical moments. For example, she went into

"Diva" from another fan favorite "Formation" on the RENAISSANCE World Tour, much to the delight of us all.

In 2015, Beyoncé performed a tribute to Stevie Wonder at an evening hosted by the Grammys in his honor. Beyoncé delivered a flawless medley of some of Stevie Wonder's biggest hits, including, "Higher Ground," "Fingertips," and "Master Blaster (Jammin')." During the performance, Beyoncé was joined by Ed Sheeran and Gary Clark Jr. While both of those artists added their own flair to the performance, it was hard to take your eyes off Beyoncé. That same year she headlined the Made in America Festival in Philadelphia.[14] Throughout the set, Beyoncé paired her own empowering anthems with famous quotes from fellow vocal feminists. We heard Ronda Rousey's verbal clap back at what she calls "do nothing bitches" because you cannot be a diva while "doing nothing," something we need to hold ourselves accountable for. Eartha Kitt's humorous reaction to the laughable suggestion that she compromise for a man was played after "Survivor," and Maya Angelou's poem "Phenomenal Woman" was played during an interlude before "Grown Woman." She also included Chimamanda Ngozi Adichie's definition of feminism in the performance of "***Flawless."

In 2016, Beyoncé went global again with the Formation World Tour. I was freshly out of college in a new city, and I was still learning and navigating the emotional and financial instability that most people in their early twenties (and beyond) experience. A friend of mine with whom I only talk about Beyoncé was going through much of the same thing and trying to make it as a dancer. As soon as *Lemonade* dropped, I began saving for the inevitable tour, which sure enough was soon announced. London's Wembley Stadium is a huge venue, my friend is very rarely on time, neither of us could afford seated tickets, and I am four foot seven inches tall. All of this led to the two of us finding ourselves somewhere in the center of the standing crowd trying to catch glimpses of Beyoncé's feet. Despite our restricted view, it was an amazing live performance. I am convinced that at one point Beyoncé looked at me. My friend disagreed and unfortunately I am unable to track down any camera footage to prove it, but I felt her eyes on me at one specific moment and did not get a cold or a pimple for a year afterward.

Another relevant fact to my Formation World Tour experience is that the friend whom I attended the show with had been through a natural-hair journey during our final year of university. Some of this journey had involved her sitting on the floor of my bedroom/living room/kitchen with cheap straightening irons that should never have touched a single strand of her amazing hair. Other parts of her journey included her sending selfies with her hair in braids, curls, or coils. In these images she would be beaming and so proud of herself. At this point in her journey, she would often choose to straighten her hair when going "out out" or when professional photos would be taken. I was on the way to Wembley Stadium when I received a selfie of her. She was in a matching Ivy Park set with her hair out—as was I. To bear witness to my friend having the most wonderful time dancing with her hair out and completely product-free was a beautiful sight that I will never forget. My friend looks amazing whatever she decides to do with hair—we all look amazing whatever we decide to do with our hair—but I cried when I saw the way her hair jumped with her to the music and again when I saw her laughing while picking confetti out of her curls on the way home. She posted a picture from the event before we had left the stadium, no filter or straighteners in sight.

A space in which we can exist in whatever way we want to be is not a given for Black women. The fact that my friend felt able to be her authentic self symbolizes the freedom and prioritization of Black womanhood present in *Lemonade* and the Formation World Tour. I was pleased to learn that it was not just me and my friend who felt this. In fact, Beyoncé played a video on stage of a fan discussing excitedly how she was going to wear her hair to the concert, stating that people who don't like natural hair can "stay mad." In true Beyoncé fashion she projected the words "stay mad" onto the back of the stage and stood in front of them.

If *Lemonade* explored and showcased the beautiful and multifaceted aspects of Black womanhood, then the Formation World Tour expanded on it. In the show we attended, she opened with "Formation," inviting the audience to yell affirmations at themselves. Immediately audiences were greeted by phenomenal Black dancers with a variety of natural hairstyles. Beyoncé presented as sexy as well as angry and in love, while poetry and visuals were weaved seamlessly with the choreography. The visuals of the dancers with Yoruba face painting in the bus from the *Lemonade* film were displayed during the show. The audience was also treated to footage of Blue Ivy and Jay-Z. These visuals gave fans a highly sought insight into her personal life and highlighted that being a Black woman is political. As journalist Hermione Hoby noted when she reviewed the tour, "The lemonade that she's making in her 34th year isn't just from the bitter juice of her famous husband's infidelities, it's the pain of black mothers and grandmothers and their mothers"; this fact was illustrated on the tour in everything from Beyoncé's home footage to the outfits.[15]

She performed "Daddy Lessons" with her Black dancers dressed in Black Panther–themed outfits. This is where I believe Beyoncé began her mission of reclaiming country music by placing it next to Blackness rather than in opposition to it. She also performed "Single Ladies" with the signature choreography from the music video, before continuing the theme of empowerment by performing "Irreplaceable" alongside the beautiful poetry of Warsan Shire. This show truly gave us everything, including her performing "Naughty Girl" and asking where the sexy ladies are in a red latex body suit. She also included an ode to Prince with footage of him performing his most famous hit, "Purple Rain," and footage of him performing with Beyoncé. The tour, like the *Lemonade* album, takes us though every stage of grief and love, holding our hands the whole way. The show we attended in the

Formation World Tour ended with her performing the rallying cry "Freedom" with water on the stage followed by the upbeat songs "End of Time" and "Halo." The audience was shown that the joy and love in "Halo" exists on the stage next to, not despite, the struggle displayed in "Freedom."

Something about this tour allowed me to dance with the complete inhibition that I have been chasing ever since. This was a tour of freedom, of confidence, and of celebrating the beauty and complexity of Black womanhood. This tour was a celebration of Beyoncé and her audience. There was a song for everyone regardless of where you were in your personal journey and how long you had been a fan. The entire show was a masterful exploration of vulnerability and power, sexuality and independence, while showcasing her skill as a live performer. It was a continuation of the empowerment she invites us all to find in *Lemonade*.

A year after the Formation World Tour she performed once again at the Grammy Awards.[16] She performed some of the ballads from *Lemonade* such as "Love Drought" and "Sandcastles." As I mentioned previously, for this performance she was dressed in gold and was heavily pregnant with her twins. Aside from the themes of motherhood in this performance, this gentle and vulnerable side of Beyoncé was stunning to see. This performance also exhibited strength in this vulnerability juxtaposed to the power of songs like "Formation." Every emotion deserves a place on the stage, and while Beyoncé belting out a ballad on stage is nothing new, this performance with its high artistic concept and a heavily pregnant Beyoncé was mystical and divine. Opening with a prerecorded spoken-word piece, this performance incorporated visual elements and other artistic mediums. When I look back at this performance it's easy to only remember the leaning-chair stunt, but I think this short performance is in fact a crucial chapter in the book of Beyoncé performances. There is something so beautiful about watching the superstar we have seen strut in hot pants to pop bangers sing slow and bluesy renditions of heartbreaking ballads. If we need evidence that

Beyoncé can turn every stage of life into art and always turn out a performance, then this is it. Also, her crown looked like a sunbeam.

While there is a wealth of detail to explore and historical significance about Beychella (the name given to Beyoncé's headlining performance at Coachella), it also represented a shift in terms of Beyoncé's live performances and what she can do with the stage. When you consider the fact that she was the first Black woman to headline Coachella and the themes she brought to the stage, it is easy to see why this performance had such a large impact. You cannot discuss the elevation of Beyoncé's live performances without discussing this now iconic headline set. By theming her performance around historically Black colleges, she highlighted the amazing talent there, stating that these references were "more important than flower crowns."[17] Beyoncé has pushed the boundaries of what a performance could be—in terms of talent and production value and politics also.

Beyoncé's RENAISSANCE World Tour was in 2023. The record-breaking tour grossed $579.8 million from 2,776,855 tickets sold for fifty-six shows. The tour started in Sweden's capital Stockholm on May 10, 2023, and finished in Kansas City, Missouri, on October 1, 2023.[18] It was Beyoncé's first tour since the On the Run II Tour in 2018 with her husband, Jay-Z. Could she recreate the magic of Beychella globally night after night? Yes. I saw two shows on the RENAISSANCE World Tour for many reasons, one being that when something seemingly defies everything you know about physics and the laws of what a human being can do, you need to see it again to believe it. The first concert I went to on the tour happened to me rather than being something that I watched. I remember her emerging in a beautiful gown and opening with "Dangerously in Love 2," but when I try to recall the rest of my first show, I just catch snippets and images. There was a moment where she rode a tank the colors of the Pan-African flag, and at one point she rode a flying silver horse above my head. While most of the details still elude me, I've come to the realization that the show was as much for the audience and the community she has shone a light on as it was for her. This for me is where the true power of a Beyoncé show lies. Not in what she is able to do, but in what she is able to give you to take away.

During one of the nights of the RENAISSANCE World Tour, she jokingly said "the mic is on." While her live performances breathe life into her fans, Beyoncé is still often accused of lip-synching. As mentioned, her performance at the inauguration of President Obama was especially dissected after it became apparent that she was lip-synching to a prerecorded track. I understand that we are permanently bombarded with images of celebrities' seemingly perfect lives, and seeing a singer caught in a lip-synching lie is somewhat satisfying, but the choreography and stage design (and yes, the live vocals) that she executes speak for themselves. Regardless of her status as one of the greatest performers to have ever lived, like most Black people in white spaces, Beyoncé is still subjected to critiques and skepticism about whether she is truly capable of what she has achieved. Kevin O'Keeffe claims in a piece for *The Atlantic* that Beyoncé "breaks our hearts" by lip-synching. I disagree and think it's reductive to claim to be "brokenhearted" considering she very rarely lip-syncs despite her intense choreography.[19]

While experiencing the RENAISSANCE World Tour live was a life-altering event, Beyoncé later brought the show to the big screen. Whether the viewer is someone who had the opportunity to see the show live and craves additional context to relive the experience, or someone wishing to see the show for the first time, Beyoncé consciously provides for her fans. This is especially significant considering the rise in ticket prices. Capturing the show brilliantly, film versions of the performances offer all fans access instead of a select few. Through films such *Homecoming* and *Renaissance: A Film by Beyoncé*, Beyoncé has shared her tours through film releases. These films provide insight into the production and the intention for each tour. Viewers see how hard Beyoncé works on her live performances, being involved in every aspect from the lighting to the crucial fan placement on stage. Every performance documentary of Beyoncé's has given me greater appreciation for the performance while feeling connected to the more intimate parts of the preparation. Viewers can see Beyoncé in her role as a creative director, which range from funny moments such as Beyoncé demanding her notes from a dress rehearsal are applied and reminding her production team that "I'm a Black girl. You can't put blue lights on Black girls."[20] Also, who can forget her manager (otherwise known as her daughter Blue Ivy Carter) informing her during the tour documentary that she *cannot* cut "Diva" from the RENAISSANCE World Tour set list.[21]

If Beyoncé consistently raises the game, then the nearly three-hour, seven-act masterpiece that is the COWBOY CARTER Tour sits proudly on top of the iconic performances that predated it. The set design was integral and embraced classic American iconography and rodeo symbolism with a star-shaped stage. Similarly to the RENAISSANCE World Tour, she offered different couture outfits and guest acts to keep the internet interested throughout the entirety of the COWBOY CARTER Tour. We also got a chance to thank Blue Ivy's management for keeping "Diva" on the set list when she returned to the stage. As a fan, and a long-term fan at that, I felt something like a victory lap in the COWBOY CARTER Tour. In addition to the celebration of Black history and country music, Beyoncé sang mash-ups that we've come to love with larger-than-life visuals that deserve a cinema release of their own (including Beyoncé as a four-hundred-foot cowboy). Unlike her earlier performances, she had nothing to prove, and she wasn't telling us who she is—she's reminding us.

From performing in front of a large rendition of her name at the BET Awards in 2003 to performing at the global giant of a tour that was RENAISSANCE, Beyoncé has dominated live performances and constantly raised the game. She not only excelled in the classic expectations of 1990s performances (and wardrobes), but she has continued to sell out stadiums and create social media–ready moments in the streaming era. Beyoncé has gone on to execute innovative artistry and has undoubtedly earned her legendary status on stages and in studios. Anyone who has watched one of her tour documentaries will know that Beyoncé is involved in everything. She will always have notes, and they *will* be applied. Her attention to detail extends from what the crew are wearing to the lighting, because she is right, you cannot put blue lights on a Black girl.

I've heard Beyoncé referred to as a force of nature regarding her live performances, but I don't think that description is fair. While her talent plays a part, I think the truth of why her live performances are as stunning as they are is way more linked to the hard work and dedication and artistic vision of those involved. The tour documentaries detail the lengthy rehearsals process, the large team, and the very clear artistic vision that goes into making a Beyoncé show happen. Beyoncé has an unparalleled ability to execute the highest vocal performances while pulling off almost unbelievable choreography. Everything about a Beyoncé show is intentional, like her and her dancers wearing red outfits designed by Black designers for Juneteenth. So no, I don't think Beyoncé's shows are a result of her being a "force of nature"—I think the truth is much simpler, yet frustrating; they are the result of her and her team's hard work. From the Beyoncé Experience tour in 2007 to her recent stadium global tours, a Beyoncé concert is always the result of a great team and a whole lot of rehearsal.

CHANGING THE GAME—
BEYONCÉ'S CONTINUED IMPACT ON THE INDUSTRY

In 2024, Stevie Wonder presented an award to Beyoncé. This wasn't a Grammy, and it wasn't related to a specific album. It was the Innovator Award presented at the iHeartRadio Music Awards. During his speech, Stevie Wonder spoke highly of Beyoncé, specifically noting that she changed the world of music forever when she released her self-titled album digitally and with no promotion. He also mentioned that she was the first African American woman to headline Coachella. This specific list of attributes was about not just her talent, voice, or dancing ability but also her impact on the industry. She received this award because of how she has used and continues to use her talent to change music and culture.[1]

Beyoncé has had a long and successful career, a point music critics and journalists often make when discussing her.[2] She has the most simultaneous Billboard hits by a woman and is the most nominated woman in Grammy history. It is true that the length of her career and her awards are to be commended, but I think what is more notable is her ability to consistently innovate her sound and influence the music industry. From providing the blueprint in how to go solo after being in a girl group, to completely reinventing how fame works in the streaming era, Beyoncé has always had innovation in her career. As someone who struggles with change, I find this aspect of what she has achieved striking. I don't like moving houses for fear I'll leave some part of me behind. I really don't like that feeling when I look around and notice something is different. But watching her accept this Innovator Award convinced me that change is fine; its value is all about how you respond to it. After all, what is innovation if not embracing the beauty of change?

One aspect of the music industry that Beyoncé has innovated is the sound of music itself. While not the first or only person to use it, Beyoncé is largely credited by music critics for the invention of the staccato rap-singing style that has become popular in pop, R & B, and hip-hop genres. She first used this technique during her time with Destiny's Child, particularly on the song "Soldier" and throughout the album *The Writing's on the Wall*. This percussive and sharp sound subsequently became increasingly popular throughout the music industry in the first decade of the 2000s, arguably becoming the new sound of R & B and revolutionizing both singing and rapping. The staccato rap-singing style was implemented by many popular artists including Drake and Kanye West. The phenomenon of mumble rappers, who saw widespread success in the late 2010s, utilized the staccato rap-singing cadence. American academic Michael Eric Dyson stated that Beyoncé "changed the whole genre" with the proliferation of rap-singing, adding: "She doesn't get credit for the remarkable way in which she changed the musical vocabulary of contemporary art."[3] With her distinctive, fast, almost hiccupping vocal technique, she has taken music in a new direction.

Another and perhaps more defining way Beyoncé has asserted herself and set herself apart is in the unannounced digital drop. In the early hours on the thirteenth of December 2013, after a relatively long period of silence and inactivity from Beyoncé, we were blessed with a full visual album, *Beyoncé*. It simply arrived online. There was no promotion before the release, no press tour, no lead single. While we did not get Beyoncé on a couch talking to Wendy Williams about what the album meant to her, we did receive fourteen songs with music videos for all. The impact of the digital drop on the industry and artists is almost immeasurable. For example, in 2014 we saw artists such as U2, Skrillex, and others also experimenting with their own version of the surprise drop. By 2016 this way of releasing an album had almost become the standard. For example, Frank Ocean's albums *Endless* and *Blonde* and Rihanna's *Anti* all arrived with minimal promotion. Even Kanye West released *The Life of Pablo* with little promotion, which is surprising considering how he usually conducts himself. Beyoncé has, it seems, almost made it uncool to promote an album, instead letting the work speak for itself. Her self-titled album generated over a million tweets in a matter of hours, and Stevie Wonder claimed she changed the world of music "forever" with this release. And no one knew a thing about it until the order link showed up on their social media timelines after its surprise midnight release.

Traditionally, albums were released on Tuesdays. However, following the surprise release of *Beyoncé*, Friday releases became the standard, because it turns out people will listen when you're Beyoncé. Cady Lang for *Time* notes how "the record industry made a collective decision in 2015 to release albums worldwide on Fridays, to have more uniform distribution and to crack down on piracy, a decision that almost certainly was spurred by Beyoncé's release."[4] This release turned the single-dominated market on its head. Her self-titled album was released with no advance single, instead demanding listeners to consume it all at once. The surprise set featured an impressive array of cutting-edge collaborators, including a pair of guest appearances from "rising stars" Drake and Frank Ocean, and another loved-up Jay-Z collab on the hit "Drunk in Love." *Beyoncé* is a cohesive body of work, and even the singles that did go on to become fan favorites sound so much better in the context of the album. In recent years, current pop stars like Charli XCX focus more on cohesive albums rather than single pop smashes with tons of radio play. In her documentary, *Life Is But a Dream*, Beyoncé laments that people "don't make albums anymore"; instead they just "try to sell a bunch of quick singles."[5] She's played a part in recertifying the issue by continuing to make full bodies of work like *Lemonade* and *The Lion King: The Gift*.

Beyoncé has also found a way to dominate the industry even with its increasing reliance on social media and streaming with her self-titled album and iconic and viral music videos like "Single Ladies." The way we consume music has changed, with so many of us now hearing a song for the first time as part of a thirty-second video on TikTok. While Beyoncé remains dedicated to creating full bodies of work, she is also excelling on social media. After all, who would have predicted that some of the most loved and quoted snippets of music in history would not arrive by way of a pop-princess chorus but by a Beyoncé ad-lib as she grunts "surfbort" on "Drunk in Love." You'd also be hard-pressed to find an internet-savvy person in America who has not posted a selfie with the caption "I woke up like this" or bought a mug printed with the word "Flawless" written in pink.[6] Beyoncé has loosened up her delivery too in a way that highlights her elasticity and shows her pop-cultural antenna tuned to the right channels, allowing for these stream-worthy hooks and verses. My friends and I often refer to the internet as "Beyoncé's internet," and even though Beyoncé rose to fame in the early 2000s, this is most certainly true. When we say it is her internet, we mean that regardless of how much she posts on it, she dominates online discussion and can go viral from a simple selfie, should she wish. She does take part in internet and meme culture, utilizing its ability to spread her message and promote her music, but she has not fallen into its cheap, dehumanizing traps. We see what she wants us to see because she dominates the internet rather than it dominating her.

Another period of elevation and innovation came in Beyoncé's *Lemonade* era. This album was, arguably, where she started more explicitly playing with genres. Michael Eric Dyson refers to the rigid music genres and the way they disproportionately impact Black artists as "artistic apartheid."[7] *Lemonade* began to push these boundaries with rock influences in "6 Inch" and country references in "Daddy Lessons." With *Lemonade* also came the tributes to the Black Lives Matter movement, and she began to be more vocal about America's racial hierarchy, which is still novel in the pop world. When Beyoncé performed "Formation" at the Super Bowl, flanked by dancers in black berets with Afros, the conservative media began to berate not only the new song, but Beyoncé as a person. Predictably, but frustratingly, many misconstrued the messages and labeled Beyoncé as radical or "anti-police." One sheriff even audaciously linked the song to the murder of police officers.[8] In this moment Beyoncé responded in a unique and unexpected way. In true Beyoncé style, she did not tweet or go on a chat show to explain herself as many celebrities would do—she just sold "Boycott Beyoncé" merch on her website. She announced the Formation World Tour in a commercial immediately following the performance. This was, amazingly, the first-ever stadium tour to be headlined by a female artist. From this so-called controversy came one of the most meaningful bodies of art in the twenty-first century and a history-making stadium tour.

RENAISSANCE was more traditionally marketed than *Beyoncé* and even *Lemonade*. It was publicized over a month in advance with Beyoncé being featured in a June 2022 *Vogue* cover story and with the release of the single "BREAK MY SOUL."[9] Again, Beyoncé utilized the internet. She produced songs that were beloved by fans *and* viral on TikTok ahead of the album release. For example, "CUFF IT" went viral in 2022 and 2023 and ultimately became the longest-running Billboard Hot 100 solo hit of her career.[10] Both the album and the world tour demonstrated how her live performances have changed to meet the demands of the streaming era. A great example of her flexing her online dominance is her "mute challenge." A lyric in "ENERGY" sees Beyoncé talk about how everybody around her is so awed that they are effectively on mute. During the RENAISSANCE World Tour fans took it upon themselves to stay as quiet as possible after the lyric until Beyoncé continued the song. On the surface it may not seem like much of a task to simply be quiet, but getting a stadium full of excited, adrenaline-filled fans to be quiet was indeed a mission for everyone in the audience who took the challenge seriously. Soon enough funny videos emerged online of fans telling other fans to "shh." Beyoncé actively engaged with the challenge by extending the pause before she carried on with the song and telling audiences how well they had done, even announcing winners and including the challenge in *Renaissance: A Film by Beyoncé*. This fun challenge highlighted Beyoncé's ability to remain relevant. Her willingness to evolve alongside the changing music industry and to embrace new ideas and practices have set her apart as a leader in the industry. From Friday releases to TikTok challenges, Beyoncé exists as a veritable trendsetter. The RENAISSANCE World Tour had a significant impact on the US economy. Yelp, *Forbes*, and *Fortune* noted that many businesses local to her tour venues, including nail salons, transportation companies, and hotels, experienced a boost thanks to the tour.[11] *Forbes* wrote how Beyoncé "reinvigorates the destinations and cultures that inspire her, leaving an indelible mark on economies, heritage, and global travel itself"—an impact otherwise known as the Beyoncé effect.[12] This testifies that not only can Beyoncé change the game, but she does so while continuing to sell out stadiums and achieve unrivalled success.

In 2016 Beyoncé performed the song "Daddy Lessons" from her *Lemonade* album at the Country Music Association Awards. She performed it with the Chicks, and as a girl from Houston with a country song on her latest album, this performance made total sense. It was stunning with great vocals from the band and of course Beyoncé. It was particularly notable because it saw Beyoncé enter the country space alongside the Chicks, who have their own history with country music. Over their career the band had a harder time breaking into the industry when compared to their male counterparts. In 2003 they received damaging backlash following their public critiques of the Iraq War and President George W. Bush.[13] After going on a hiatus in 2008, the band reunited in 2016 to go on tour. While the performance at the Country Music Awards was praised by some viewers and critics, some country stars and fans disagreed with the praise. Many claimed Beyoncé wasn't a country artist and had no business at the award show, leading to racist backlash online. Beyoncé did not take to social media or release a statement. Instead, she got her team together and went to the studio. In 2024, eight years after the "Daddy Lessons" performance, Beyoncé attended the Grammys in a large and striking white cowboy hat. For those like me who were at that time speculating what would follow *RENAISSANCE*, this served as confirmation the next album would be country. Not only was it a country album, but it was an album that hosted a conversation about the very idea of genres and about Black artists' place within them.

When Stevie Wonder gave her the Innovator Award, she had just released the genre-bending country-as-hell album *COWBOY CARTER*. The album features the voice of Black country legend Linda Martell, who opens "SPAGHETTII," which can most accurately be called a rap-country song. At the start of the song Martell expresses that genres are confining rather than in service to art and in fact shackle artists rather than champion their creative freedom. Martell, who is featured on two songs on the album, was the first female Black artist to be in the Top 25 on the Billboard Country Music Charts in 1969. She was the highest-charting Black woman for over twenty-five years, until Beyoncé's "TEXAS HOLD 'EM" reached number one, and she was the first Black woman to perform at the Grand Ole Opry. However, during her career she endured racist abuse and was blackballed in the music industry by the owner of Plantation Records, which she left because of its name. *Rolling Stone* named her country's "Lost Pioneer."[14]

Linda Martell is not the only country legend on *COWBOY CARTER*. During Willie Nelson's interlude "SMOKE HOUR ★

WILLIE NELSON," someone is flipping through radio stations (all the interludes imitate a radio broadcast) as snippets of "Grinnin' in Your Face" by Son House, "Down by the Riverside" by Sister Rosetta Tharpe, "Maybellene" by Chuck Berry, and "Don't Let Go" performed by Roy Hamilton play. These Black artists were pioneers in their respective genres, but their place in history has been whitewashed. In these features and interludes of pure Black talent, the true message of *COWBOY CARTER* becomes apparent. The album aims to undo the erasure of Black country artists. It forced listeners to see the red blood in America's red, white, and blue flag. The idea of blending genres, or reclaiming them, is one of the most drastic ways Beyoncé has altered the music industry. With *Lemonade*, *RENAISSANCE*, and *COWBOY CARTER*, she has been recovering genres that Black women pioneered but have not been afforded space in.

After *COWBOY CARTER* was released and began to break records with its explicit commentary on genres, the Country Music Awards snubbed the album by not nominating it for any awards at the 2024 award show. Despite its success and undeniably country sound, it was still "not allowed" in this space. However, Beyoncé's lyrics often argue that the best revenge is success, and true to form, one year after attending the Grammys in a wide-brimmed cowboy hat, she returned to collect the Best Country Album Award for *COWBOY CARTER*. This was also the year she finally took home the Grammy for Album of the Year—better late than never. Beyoncé makes her point through the art itself. As Tamara Palmer wrote for the Grammys online, Beyoncé not only "bends" genres with this album, but she also serves up a "poignant response to naysayers" who have sought to exclude her, and Blackness in general, from country music.[15]

Beyoncé remains, and has always been, steadfastly committed to pushing forward in pursuit of great art and entertainment. She does not chase trends or youth, though she does have a habit of starting trends seemingly unintentionally. Even when collaborating with newer artists such as Megan Thee Stallion, she can meet them on common ground that does not result in either party being compromised, contorted, or appearing inauthentic. Instead, Beyoncé only seems to chase greatness and remains fully committed to producing realized artistic projects that will add to her legacy and the history of popular music more broadly. There are no flop eras for her, no periods where she disappeared for a half decade, no clear mistakes that were not immediately rectified. There are only varying degrees of winning for over two decades. Beyoncé excels at creating changes while still sounding like herself. Other artists go through phases, often shallow and short lived, but every album of hers has been an authentic Beyoncé album.

When accepting the Innovator of the Year Award from Stevie Wonder, Beyoncé spoke about how she hopes that we will be more open to artists who create shifts. She thanked other artists that defy any labels placed on them and hoped for more openness to the joy and liberation that comes from enjoying art with no preconceived notions.[16] It was a speech that expressed her belief that everyone should be able to creatively adapt. In watching her speech, I thought about how Beyoncé has certainly elevated live performances, but she has also changed so much how artists and the music industry function. Whether it is redefining genres or changing how albums are released, Beyoncé's career is one of elevation and innovation. With albums like *The Lion King: The Gift* and *Lemonade* she has broken the post-racial myth that so often follows successful Black people. She changed what the music industry thought possible when she released her self-titled visual album as a surprise. She made Friday releases the standard and continues to utilize social media while not falling into its traps. This is even more impressive when we remember that she became famous at a time when many of the current mediums she now dominates did not even exist. Despite being famous since the 1990s, she has met the unique challenges of the TikTok thirty-second-clip era of music. I may be biased, but I truly think that no one else can innovate and excel so continuously in such a changing industry.

When music journalists and magazines discuss Beyoncé's greatness, they often note the length of her career, her Grammys, or her headline sets. She has continued to outrival and command the streaming era, and that requires large amounts of innovation. However, it is in the art itself (not just the accolades) that the true transformation lies. It is in a tour that can make us all question what it is to be American, and it is in the songs that break the boundaries.[17] I think we often get stuck in a version of ourselves, and change is scary, but we can learn from how Beyoncé has used reinvention not simply to stay relevant but to elevate, tell new stories, and reclaim musical genres stolen from Black people.

"BEYONCÉ?!"—THE CELEBRITY'S CELEBRITY

For someone as invested in popular culture as I am, one of my more hypocritical opinions is that I think we all know too much about celebrities. In recent years, there's been a shift in celebrity culture with social media and friendly anecdotes on late-night talk shows, creating the illusion we are connected. Celebrities now participate in interviews where they show what is in their handbag, contents that are always perfectly curated and strike the balance between aspirational and relatable. I've seen tours of celebrity houses with living rooms that are obnoxiously large but disingenuously described as "homely" and full of "character." After all, nothing says authenticity like an artificial brick wall. For a lot of celebrities I like, I know too much about the interior of their (posed) living room, their favorite eye cream, who their nail tech is. YouTube turned into social media, interviews turned into tweets, tweets turned into videos, and now we are simply inundated with information on celebrities. As cynical as I may sound, I do not think all these insights are inherently bad, but this shift arguably does create unhealthy parasocial relationships between celebrities and their fans, with celebrities centered around a myth of intimacy.

However, this is distinctly not the case with Beyoncé. As the Hive knows all too well, to be a fan of Beyoncé is to get what you are occasionally given. Beyoncé rarely does interviews and is very sparse about what she reveals on social media. While much can be said about how unique her music is, the way she conducts herself is almost as unique. Even though she has been in the public eye for most of her life, she is now a relatively private person. This persona is very different from how she conducted herself during the earlier portions of her career. In the 1990s and early 2000s she would do interviews with Destiny's Child and after she went solo. She has even sat with Tyra Banks and joked with her about a cardboard cutout of Jay-Z.[1] However, her public appearances have vastly decreased, and we now get very little of these moments. This mystique and quiet celebrity adds to the idolization of her. There are many factors that contribute to the air around Beyoncé, and one is that she does not chase the relatability factor as other celebrities do. We know very little about her life, and it is a running joke that she stays in her house. This is because she has instead followed the air of old-school Hollywood celebrities, which in turn leads the fans to fill in the blanks.

This expertly crafted privacy also translates into how she uses the ever-growing medium of social media. She joined Twitter and Instagram in 2012, utilizing these sites to engage with her fan base. She has a large but very curated social media presence, which means that most of what we know about her, or think we know about her, comes from her art itself. Many celebrities share snippets of their home life on social media; however, we don't receive this from Beyoncé. Instead, she posts occasional photos, usually at events. In fact, in 2025 fans were waiting for her to post images from the notorious Grammys after-party. Again, with Beyoncé you get what you are given, and it is much better to have fans begging for pictures rather than becoming bored of seeing them.

Rather than post footage of herself and her family on Instagram, she will instead often share these images in black and white on a screen as part of her tour visuals. We may not have been given a photograph of Blue Ivy's first meal, but we did get a hilarious clip of Blue Ivy informing her mother that she cannot cut "Diva" from her RENAISSANCE World Tour set list. Instead of maintaining a high social media presence at every turn, she shares moments from Blue Ivy's childhood, images from her wedding, and holiday pictures alongside her art. Ultimately, she wants fans to consume and invest in art. More intimate images are used to illuminate the message of the music, not just to accumulate "likes." This makes what she does share feel more authentic and rare, adding to their meaning in the public imagination and turning them into a wider performance rather than more meaningless celebrity content.

A major shift in how Beyoncé engages with fans came not only when she joined social media in 2012, but also when she made the documentary *Life Is But a Dream* in 2013.[2] The project was the culmination of an entire career's worth of archive footage and photographs kept in a digital storage room in the Knowles' offices. Since 2005, Beyoncé has used a visual director to film her life and has used a video camera on her personal computer. Bey is known for insisting on privacy, and the media hailed the film as a rare glimpse into her private life. This included the events of her marriage to Jay-Z and her miscarriage prior to the birth of Blue Ivy. In the film, she discusses her journey to motherhood, including comedic clips of how she hid her baby bump from the public. The film also explores professional moments such as her split from her father, Mathew Knowles, as her manager. Speaking during the film she says, "I always battle with: How much do I reveal about myself? How do I keep my humility? How do I keep my spirit and the reality? And how do I continue to be generous to—to my fans and to my craft? And how do I stay current? But how do I stay soulful? And it is the battle of my life. When I walk onto a stage I'm able to come out of my shell and be as fabulous and over the top and strong and powerful as I want to be."[3] It's fair to say that this is a "battle" she has won time and time again, with

Beyoncé always revealing just enough. For example, she will post a cryptic image on Instagram, letting her fans argue among themselves about whether she will ever release the *RENAISSANCE* visuals. She makes us speculate by dropping hints and letting us set our own expectations. She has expertly walked a tightrope between revealing only what she is comfortable with sharing and giving her fans information that they are so desperate for.

There is humor in the privacy Beyoncé implores as a celebrity, which is shown in the *I Am... World Tour* documentary.[4] In this film she includes footage of her shopping at a mall. Onlookers were following her around a department store as she was shopping, and her crew interviewed several of them about why they were fans of Beyoncé and what she meant to them. One fan the team spoke to was annoyed that she had not said hello to him. He even called her a bitch to her own camera crew. Later in the documentary there is more footage of her shopping, including moments where she says hello to that exact same fan. The team interviewed him after he met her, and he then gushed about how much he loves her, completely backtracking on his earlier assessment. The camera crew discreetly say "if only she knew" as the fan continues to smile. In true Beyoncé style, she included the entire interaction in the documentary.

Beyoncé: Year of 4 is another documentary that similarly uses home footage to document the personal journey that led to the album *4*. The film shows Beyoncé taking time for herself to travel and pick her nephew up from school, before concluding that she is not the same Beyoncé that emerged from Destiny's Child. She was going through a process of evolution, and so was her art. We see her scuba diving and walking along the Great Wall of China. The process of deciding to manage herself is also shown, a move she describes as risky. Despite the risk, she aims to set the example that she can own and run her own business as a woman. She discusses her work ethic, what she does before she goes to sleep, and what it's like managing herself. We follow her from rehearsal rooms to meetings and photo shoots in Paris, as well as when she receives flowers from Jay-Z. These films are how Beyoncé shares personal information with the public, on her own terms.[5] *Beyoncé: Year of 4* wasn't salacious clickbait, and it didn't pander to gossip. It was a plea for all women to reach for the stars and do what they need to reach their full potential.

For someone who doesn't talk in public that much, Beyoncé is very good at cracking jokes. After fans begged and pleaded for the *RENAISSANCE* visuals, she took her Halloween photos in front of a mock backdrop for the "MTV No Visuals Awards" and posted them on social media. The comments from fans were as hilarious as the joke itself, with many loving how Beyoncé was essentially trolling her fans. Beyoncé is not the type of celebrity to tell a funny story to an interviewer, or go on TikTok to share an embarrassing anecdote, but that does not mean she does not make us laugh on a regular basis. Another funny moment came when she was about to perform live on Netflix for *A Cowboy Carter Christmas*. Netflix had hosted a live sporting event shortly before, and the high demand meant that for many the buffered streaming interrupted their viewing. Due to this misstep, fans online were worrying about the streaming platform's ability to keep up with the demand and the large number of people who would be tuning in to see Beyoncé. Many made the point that the Hive can be demanding and would not cope well with buffering interruptions of the performance. In response, Beyoncé posted a teaser video on Instagram that stalled and appeared to be buffering, again trolling fans and Netflix.

Anyone who watched the 2024 Grammy Awards will know that the event turned into a Beyoncé meet and greet. During breaks at the ceremony, celebrities (many of whom were being celebrated themselves that night) queued up to meet and take a photo with Beyoncé. While being a comical moment for fans like myself, it also revealed something that followers of Beyoncé have known for a while—she is the celebrities' celebrity. It was fascinating to see people who have achieved immense success be completely starstruck upon meeting her. Comedian, commentator, and Grammy host Trevor Noah, who met and took a photo with Beyoncé, even spoke about it on his podcast.[6] Despite hosting the awards and achieving his own career highlights that night, he was still asked about meeting Beyoncé. Further cementing her status as the celebrities' celebrity, both Michelle Obama and Kamala Harris congratulated her on the release of *COWBOY CARTER* and its messaging around Black women's place in country music.[7]

The best example of Beyoncé differing from other celebrities in terms of how she navigates being a celebrity is how she handled the drama over not being nominated for a Country Music Association Award for her album *COWBOY CARTER*. Beyoncé handled the situation quietly and deliberately, letting the messaging from the album speak for itself.[8] The first song on the album even asks the question explicitly, what's more country than the way she has built her life and career? Her reaction to the racism from the wider country music community and their erasure of not only herself but Black talent more broadly is quintessentially Beyoncé. She did not go on an Instagram tirade or demand a seat at the table. Instead, she made her own table by creating an album that cemented her voice in the country space so undeniably that the arguments about the lack of her award nomination became reductive. *COWBOY CARTER* itself is arguably a response to her being previously snubbed by the Country Music Awards.

In this climate of over-familiarity, Beyoncé reveals very little about her private life. By keeping us out of the more personal aspects of her life, Beyoncé is someone who, in the eyes of her fans, transcends human limitations. Beyoncé has cultivated an almost divine status in pop culture, mainly because there is a huge amount of power in the unknown. My friend tells me that a crush is simply a lack of information, and this enigma of Beyoncé is certainly intoxicating. This larger-than-life yet unknowable persona is so attractive in the modern celebrity age. It's not about what she chooses to share—it's about what she does not share, and how that choice gives her a unique level of agency for such an A-list star. Her carefully curated public image leaves so much space for mystery and speculation, and this mystery is a form of power. Beyoncé is a living paradox, both omnipresent and unknowable, a perfect statement on the limitations of celebrity in the social media age.

THE INNOVATION OF BEYONCÉ'S DICTIONARY

Beyoncé's cultural impact expands beyond music, especially when considering her contribution to language, both offline and on social media. When I attended Black Pride in 2023 in London, I saw a stall selling large handheld paper fans. People were buying the fans to keep themselves cool, but also because they featured gorgeous designs. The fans were printed with words in a large font that were revealed as you opened your fan. There were fans that read "Black Lives Matter" and "Black and Proud," while others featured famous Beyoncé phrases. One read "These Karens are terrorists," and another simply said "Thique," both referring to *RENAISSANCE* lyrics. The fan I chose to purchase was printed with "Call Becky," a quintessential reference to *Lemonade*. As I looked at these fans and the gorgeous people buying and using them, I was reminded that the messages printed on them were more than lyrics; they were an expression that Black is beautiful and exemplified Beyoncé's global impact. *Forbes* describe Beyoncé as a global tastemaker, and this impact does not stop at music and fashion—it extends into language.[1]

To paraphrase Linda Martell, language is a funny little concept. Language has rules we all consciously or unconsciously abide by. It is constantly evolving, and the impact of Beyoncé's career is apparent in the words and phrases she irrevocably adds into the public lexicon. One of Beyoncé's earliest contributions to the English language was with Destiny's Child when they coined the term "bootylicious," which was subsequently added to several dictionaries.[2] It is a widely used word that celebrates a curvy and bottom-heavy body type that was mainly considered unattractive at the time of the release of "Bootylicious." This is why language in music is so important, and as we've seen with the word diva, one word can be a slur from one mouth but mean something completely different from another mouth. The Destiny's Child hit "Bug a Boo" brought the titular term into the public lexicon. In wider language, a bugaboo is a somewhat generic term to refer to something that causes fear, but in African American English, "bugaboo" can refer to a man or romantic partner who will not leave you alone. In the song, a bugaboo keeps calling and will not respect the singers' boundaries. The girls did not invent the term bugaboo but certainly made it more mainstream. Even though the phrase is very 1990s and early 2000s, I have friends who to this day will refer to an overzealous boss or too-eager man in a club as a bugaboo.[3]

Throughout Beyoncé's career, her lyrics create lasting change in popular culture. The phrase "to the left" from her 2006 song "Irreplaceable" is now commonly used to represent the dismissal of a person, particularly a cheating or disrespectful partner. It has even gained popularity through political memes. When my friend's boyfriend was disrespecting her, I simply texted, "to the left." In this context it was more than just a phrase; it was an instruction for my friend to demand nothing less than what she deserves in a language we both understand. Similarly, when Beyoncé boasted about waking up "flawless," it was not simply a declaration of her beauty, but a decree that perfection is in all of us as soon as we open our eyes in the morning.

As previously mentioned, Beyoncé popularized the controversial phrase in *Lemonade* when she instructed her cheating partner to call "Becky with the good hair." The name Becky (a form of

Rebecca) can be used as slang to describe a generic white woman considered unaware of her own privilege and prejudice.[4] Beyoncé's "Becky" from her 2016 song "Sorry" inspired memes, jokes, and much speculation, or—as Cara Kelly described it for *USA Today*—a "firestorm."[5] Many listeners questioned why Beyoncé chose to mention the name Becky specifically, but this name has a long history in popular culture. It's often been used as a generic white woman's name, associated with Sir Mix-a-Lot's 1992 "Baby Got Back," which opens with a white woman gossiping to a friend (called Becky) about a Black woman's body. Reaching even further back, Becky Sharp is a seductive social climber in William Thackeray's 1847–1848 serial novel *Vanity Fair*. In the broader context of popular culture, the name Becky is used to represent the privilege that comes with being a conventionally attractive white woman. The popularization of the phrase "Becky with the good hair" inspired overdue critiques of white womanhood. Fans took to the internet to try to work out who the "Becky" Jay-Z supposedly cheated with was and hounded several suspects online, including Rachel Roy and singer Rita Ora. As entertaining as this was, I believe that it doesn't really matter who this specific "Becky" is, because the lyric is about white womanhood being exalted and prioritized at the expense of Black woman and Black love, and that impact is bigger than one person. Ultimately, Beyoncé's use of "Becky" rejects the public adoration of white womanhood and Eurocentric beauty ideals.

Later, Beyoncé would use the name "Karen" in a similar manner. Karen is a pejorative slang term popularized in the 2020s to represent a white woman who is not only privileged but who uses this privilege to her advantage when she feels as though she has been inconvenienced. In *RENAISSANCE*, an album that is political in a less overt but still impactful way, Beyoncé declared that "Karens" are now "terrorists." Highlighting the deadly impact of Karen-like actions, Beyoncé argues that white women using their privilege at the expense of those around them is more than just something to laugh about on social media; it's a problem that creates terror. With her use of "Becky" and "Karen," Beyoncé critiques the power society awards white womanhood—and makes us all laugh at the same time.

"Karen," "bootylicious," and terms Beyoncé has coined have much more significance than one might initially think. These words and phrases are examples of how her lyrics stretch beyond music and can alter how we move through the world and how we speak to each other and ourselves. They are more than lyrics or pop culture slogans. In a world that has a plethora of language to disrespect Black women, Beyoncé has given us language that does the opposite. Whether she is posting a picture declaring how she "woke up like this" or proudly calling herself "thique," her contribution to language as well as music more broadly is undeniable.

AN ODE TO THE FRIENDS I ONLY SEE TO TALK ABOUT BEYONCÉ AND THROW ASS

One thing about members of the Hive is that we are dedicated. Another is that we will find each other. This is why I have friendships entirely based on Beyoncé. I have a group chat that pretty much only comes alive when there is a Beyoncé announcement or performance. To those who are not Beyoncé fans, or those who perhaps just don't center music in their life, this may sound odd or superfluous. So, I will try to explain why I have more than one friend I only really talk to about Beyoncé. Because of the themes of her music, if you like Beyoncé, then there is a high probability you will have other qualities in common with her fellow fans.

When Beyoncé announced the COWBOY CARTER Tour my dedicated group chat came to life. It was equal parts logistical planning and excitement. We banded together to debate whether we should fly across the world and sort out city options to attend the tour. We discussed whose house we'd stay at, who had the Beyhive ticket presale code, and what we were going to wear. On the day the ticket sales opened, more accurately known to Hive members as the Beyoncé hunger games day, we were on a group call for hours. We talked to each other as we got to the front of the ticketing queue, and then subsequently were kicked out of the queue, and finally got back in the queue again. When my friend's presale code did not arrive, she told me that another friend of hers had said we could use his. After I asked how they met, she told me that they met at the RENAISSANCE World Tour. When he attended the concert on his own, they met and he joined her group where they laughed and danced together all night. I was not surprised to hear this because to be at a Beyoncé show is to bear witness to a kind of greatness that bonds people for life. To be with someone for some of their most formative memories, even if those memories are created with thousands of other people, is intimate.

What I must confess to though is that not all these Beyoncé-based friendships are close ones. Some of the people I share these friendships with are my nearest and dearest, while others I only see at concerts or for the debrief after a televised performance. For example, I have another friend who I won't speak to for ages but will occasionally send me voice notes of his imitation of Linda Martell's opening to "SPAGHETTII." Friendships are a funny little thing, aren't they? Yes, they are. I have another friend who I send outfit pictures to, but only pictures of outfits I wear to Beyoncé's concerts; it's a cherished ritual. I will send her an image of myself in denim shorts; she'll reply that they look cute but ask if I can effectively shake my ass in them. I'll tell her that they are dance approved; she'll say "sicccccckkkk." These friends may not have been at my wedding or master's graduation, but I share some of my most meaningful friendships with them.

I don't think this ode is just for Beyoncé-based friendships; I think music friendships in general are meaningful. I have a friend who has spoken about feeling the safest she has ever felt at heavy metal concerts and another friend who got over her worst breakup by dancing till 3 a.m. at raves. Music- (or Beyoncé-) based friendships are so meaningful because we all have so much more in common than our favorite artist. We all find something more in the music, something bigger than us. In the case of the Hive, we also all believe a Black woman is the greatest living entertainer, and that belief is about so much more than Beyoncé.

If you like Beyoncé, you don't just like the music; you like powerful women and excellence. She expands beyond simply being a popstar because of the themes she explores in her music, which represent much more than just herself. We are not just talking about Beyoncé when we talk about Beyoncé; we are talking about our heartbreak, about queer joy, about the reductive way genres work in the music industry, and about the beauty that is Black womanhood. So, though I have friends with whom I only talk about Beyoncé, we have talked about so much more during these conversations. So, this one's for you, the guy who sent me his Beyhive presale code when mine didn't arrive, and to you, who lied and told me I could pull off assless chaps. May we all find what we are looking for under the disco ball or hidden somewhere in an opening ballad. I love you all, so much, and I love the way we love.

NINE REASONS WHY I CRIED AT THE COWBOY CARTER TOUR

(1) Because she turned the national anthem into "Freedom."

Beyoncé is no stranger to incorporating Black politics into her music. During the first set at each night's show during the COWBOY CARTER Tour, she performed the American national anthem. Since Beyoncé is an artist who has become increasingly vocal about the United States' treatment of the Black community, it might seem like an odd choice for her to honor a country with that particular history. However, this was not a standard rendition of the anthem; it was a homage to the version Jimi Hendrix performed at Woodstock in August 1969. As the *New Yorker* compellingly argues, what Hendrix did with "The Star-Spangled Banner" was something else altogether. The article noted that this performance "was, among other things, an act of protest whose power and convincingness were inseparable from its identity as a fiercely nonconformist act of individual expression."[1] As I have stated, I think *COWBOY CARTER* is about death, and the Hendrix version of the American national anthem was also viewed as a eulogy to those young men who had lost their lives in the war in Vietnam. If her rendition of the anthem wasn't enough of a political message yelled from the stage, she then launched into "Freedom" from *Lemonade*, a song that literally and figuratively invites us to break chains. In a tour that invites us to question what America is, this was the perfect way to open her set.

(2) Because she dedicated "BLACKBIIRD" to all the Black women who have come before her.

"BLACKBIIRD" is one of the songs on *COWBOY CARTER* that immediately grabbed me. Hearing the harmonies, being introduced to some of my new favorite artists all through a cover of a song that is about women in the Civil Rights Movement was phenomenal. In one of the concerts I attended on tour, Beyoncé wore a T-shirt designed by Stella McCartney with two bedazzled blackbirds flying toward each other on her chest. It's a beautiful song on its own, but hearing it in the context of this tour took its themes to a new level entirely. Take away the production, the fans, and the choreography, and Beyoncé is a vocalist; and these vocals made her performance in a stadium feel like an intimate gig. Before she sang "BLACKBIIRD" she told us that the song was dedicated to all the Black women that have come before her. On the screen behind her she displayed images of some of these women, pioneers of music and American culture placed on the biggest stages imaginable.

(3 or Tre) Because I needed to hear an American poem.

At one point in the show, she salutes and walks off stage where a visual of her is revealed. In it, she is wearing a sash that reads "the reclamation of America." Later she plays Ras Baraka's poem that he performed on *Def Poetry Jam*. The poem is perfectly titled "American Poem." In this performance, much like Beyoncé does with the tour, Baraka questions what makes America, America. He reaches the conclusion that African Americans, including sharecroppers who are so often left out of this discussion and the

American dream, have truly made America. Ras Baraka is not only a poet but a politician known for campaigning for policies like universal basic income in Newark, New Jersey.

Beyoncé honored spaghetti westerns with the tour visuals and her song "SPAGHETTII." Spaghetti westerns are a subgenre of western films so named because of the Italian filmmakers behind them. These films often explore themes of revenge, violence, and moral ambiguity. Spaghetti western films offer a more cynical perspective than traditional Hollywood westerns, but in them there was still joy and so much love. Like spaghetti westerns, Beyoncé took what we consider to be America and turned it on its head, honoring it with this darker subgenre on the album.

(4) Because of timing.

For me the conversation about whether the RENAISSANCE World Tour was better than the COWBOY CARTER Tour is reductive. When Beyoncé toured *RENAISSANCE*, we had just come out of the COVID-19-fueled lockdown, and I needed that release and that joy of her concert. I needed to dance in sequins; I needed "BREAK MY SOUL." Beyoncé noted that *COWBOY CARTER* was meant to be act 1 prior to the release of *RENAISSANCE*. In a press release she stated, "but with the pandemic, there was too much heaviness in the world. We wanted to dance. We deserved to dance. But I had to trust God's timing."[2] *COWBOY CARTER* is a rallying cry, the start of a conversation, and as we know *RENAISSANCE* was intended to be act 2, kicking off the yet unfinished trilogy with this album would have been one hell of an opener. However, switching the release order was a perfect decision. Coming out of the lockdown to *RENAISSANCE* felt like being welcomed back into the world via the brightest of runways. It wasn't just me who felt this; as Beyoncé said, the world needed to dance.

As I'm writing this, Beyoncé is touring *COWBOY CARTER*; Trump is in office, and the world is still at the mercy of white men's egos. That is the tour I and we need right now. We need to hear Ras Baraka's poem in a stadium and needed this reclamation of what it is to be an American. As stated previously, everything about Beyoncé is intentional, including timing. The conversation *COWBOY CARTER* started was not canceled; it was just delayed—and the time to continue that conversation is now.

(5) Because of the Chitlin' Circuit.

The *COWBOY CARTER* album and the tour make constant references to the Chitlin' Circuit. The Chitlin' Circuit was a network of live entertainment venues in the US that catered to African American audiences and booked Black performers during the period of Jim Crow segregation from the early twentieth century through the 1960s. The clubs of the Chitlin' Circuit put on a variety of acts that included music, dancing, and sometimes comedy. These venues played a crucial role in popularizing blues, jazz, R & B, and rock and roll. Beyoncé has often referenced African American soul food in her music, and it was also integral to the Chitlin' Circuit. The name "Chitlin' Circuit" derives from the word "chitterlings," the term for a Southern dish consisting of pigs' intestines that are either fried or stewed with spices and all sorts of seasonings and aromatics. This has been a staple of African American food since the era of slavery because rather than simply eat the less desired ingredients and meat cuttings they were given, African Americans have consistently turned them into a delicacy. Many performance venues on the Chitlin' Circuit served chitlins and other soul food dishes, and performers were sometimes even paid with a meal instead of cash.

The impact of the circuit continues well into the present day because after the heyday of the Chitlin' Circuit, a network of Black clubs and venues continued to operate and showcase both established and new talent. As a historian, I find it wonderful to see people from all over the world paying respect to the Chitlin' Circuit, wearing references to it on their backs or just naming it during lyrics. Even if attendees of Beyoncé's concert were not aware of the history of the circuit she mentioned, the name created a unity and a club that we knew welcomed us, even if we didn't know why. I was so pleased to see Beyoncé take this crucial conversation and these historic references across the world to cities like London and Paris.

(6) Because of Rumi, Blue Ivy, and motherhood.

So much of the tour felt like a circular exploration of themes Beyoncé has investigated throughout her career. The tour represented her returning to her roots as a Texan girl and holding a mirror up to the very industry she has dominated for years. One theme during the tour was motherhood. She played home videos on screens behind her. In this footage we saw her twins as babies and Blue Ivy holding her siblings. But it wasn't just the visuals that impacted me. Blue Ivy came on stage as a professional dancer. It is always great to see Blue Ivy's talent and personality whenever we are allowed to, but during this tour we saw her excel at intricate and fully realized choreography. During the show she was on stage a lot and even has a runway moment as we hear "every queen needs an heir" in Kevin Jz Prodigy's iconic voice.[3] During the RENAISSANCE World Tour, Blue Ivy performed for a short section of each concert, but to see her talent reach this high level on the COWBOY CARTER Tour and see her blend with the fully trained adult dancers felt like I was witnessing the birth of a star.

During this tour Rumi made her onstage debut during the song "PROTECTOR." The song is a sonic act of mothering, and Beyoncé performs it with Blue Ivy sitting behind her and Rumi next to her. Given everything Black girls go through, seeing these girls be surrounded by so much love, not just from their mother but from stadiums full of people really healed something in me. The pure talent and confidence of Blue Ivy and the sheer joy on Rumi's face is a defining moment of the tour. This was more than a gimmick of inviting her kids on stage. In this context Rumi and Blue Ivy represent both legacy and the future Beyoncé is trying to improve. In a tour that explores themes that are so political and global, seeing these ultra-personal moments reminded us that these themes are not bigger than us; they are questions that we need to answer to love and heal and hold each other.

(7) Because of my fellow attendees.

If I thought people showed up and showed out for the RENAISSANCE World Tour, then they brought it to another level for the COWBOY CARTER Tour. To start, the outfits were exceptional. Cowboy hats may not be the most practical concert attire, and denim is not easy to dance in—but we made it work. I was lucky enough to stand next to members of the Brazilian Hive who had traveled to London to see the show (and the gay bars in Soho). Next to them were two stunning Black women from South Africa who had traveled for the tour and were following Beyoncé to her next stop in Paris. Being near so many people who had crossed oceans to listen to music felt validating and unifying. In *COWBOY CARTER* Beyoncé calls America a pretty house that we never settled in, and for the nearly three hours of the concert we all settled together. Differences, even in language, became irrelevant, and I am so grateful for all of those I shared the space with.

(8) Because she threw it all the way back.

In the words of a good friend of mine, the tour felt like a homage to everything Beyoncé has done and everything she will do. This is because on the tour she performed songs from *COWBOY CARTER* and *RENAISSANCE*, but she also gave us hits like "Diva" and "Irreplaceable." The inclusion of older songs gave audiences moments of sheer joy and also offered us a greater understanding of how the themes in her newer work exist throughout her entire discography. *COWBOY CARTER* isn't her first entry into country music, for she has *always* been country. Her music has *always* been American and Black and beautiful. The juxtaposition of her older songs to songs about her children offers a glimpse at a lifetime of artistry. It was a celebration of all the stages of her work, and subsequently all the stages of us.

(9) Because she didn't want to go home and neither did I.

At the end of the concert in London, which was night six of the tour, Beyoncé said that she didn't want to go home. The London audience screamed in response as we metaphorically grabbed on to her ankles while screaming "don't go" like a child with abandonment issues. During every tour she cements her status as the greatest living entertainer and offers a completely unique experience to audiences. No matter where you are in the stadium, your view is a visual feast. Beyoncé's tours establish safe and politically conscious spaces. Leaving them can feel like going back into the vulnerability of the real world.

Luckily, she leaves us with the memories, the pivotal moments captured on our phones and heart. I still feel the Formation World Tour every time my friends and I dance to a *Lemonade* track. I'm transported to the RENAISSANCE World Tour when I laugh with my queer family. I remember the imagery of the COWBOY CARTER Tour when having hard conversations with my family or reading newspapers. Poets and writers often talk about how we are a collage of our moments, how all our experiences shape a part of us and change how we navigate the world. The COWBOY CARTER Tour has found its way to the center of my collage. From now on I am avoiding nothing, I am reclaiming everything, and I am not asking for permission for what was always mine.

CONCLUSION

When I am asked why I like Beyoncé, I think of many answers. On some days I might mention specific songs or albums, "Formation," *Lemonade*, "Love on Top," and *RENAISSANCE* usually. Another day I might describe what it is like to see her perform live, the experience of being completely immersed in her talent. If I am given sufficient time, I will probably talk about the *Homecoming* film and her headlining Coachella, how she brought the rich culture of historically Black colleges onto the most mainstream of stages. Her talent, her vocals, her ballads and dance anthems—all this plays a part in why I think she is the greatest living entertainer. However, as I've interrogated my own relationship to music and to Beyoncé's work specifically, I've come to realize, and hopefully articulate, this relationship is about something much more important.

So, if I am asked about Beyoncé on a day when I am caffeinated and wanting to have a deeper conversation, I will talk about how Black women are not granted many reflections of themselves. When we do see ourselves, we are often shown images of us through a twisted mirror. The mirror Beyoncé holds up to Black women is not twisted or dark; it is rose tinted and encrusted with rhinestones. At every part of my life Beyoncé has been there. As I learned my body, developed relationships, and expanded my perception of what I can be—she has been there to put rhinestones on it all. Black women are consistently under attack, and anything that prioritizes our emotions and joy is fine by me. This is why I am a fan, because I stand taller when I hear a Beyoncé track. She walks like she has permission to be wherever she is, and I think we could all use a bit of that. The greatest performer in the world is a Black woman, and to me that is crucial. She has a talent so undeniable that everything else almost ceases to be relevant, and yet she makes her politics and feminism relevant to all her work. I am of the belief that celebrity culture and billionaires will not save or change the world. We all need more than joy, dancing, and concerts to survive. However, I do believe that music, popular culture, and the art we consume are essential in helping us find our way in this world. When so much of Black womanhood is about survival, the dancing and the joy are a much-needed breath of fresh air.

Beyoncé's music allows me to fully embrace my humanity: the messy, angry, and joyful parts of it. There is an affirmation in a Beyoncé lyric for *everything* I am. It is for these reasons that I agree with one of my favorite writers and commentators Veronica Chambers when she argues, "when the history of Black women in the twenty-first century is written, Beyoncé's place, her work as a marker for power and possibility, will be undisputable."[1] What is more undisputable is how much she has given us, the moments she has created, the language, and the radical joy. I am most grateful for dancing at a stadium when "CHURCH GIRL" dropped and seeing my friends' curls jump to the beat of "Formation."

I opened this book with a memory, and I want to close it with an invitation. I invite us all to look at what music has provided. The moments where we have turned to an artist to articulate what we are not able to, the moments where we have lost ourselves on a dance floor or in a stadium. People often talk about music as being healing; I think it's healing in the same way water is—essential and part of the very essence of what makes us human. All of this to say thank you, Beyoncé, for reflecting my humanity back to me with the most fabulous of mirrors.

ACKNOWLEDGMENTS

I want to thank my wife, Olivia Powell, first and foremost. I want to thank her for the day-to-day, everything from the warm cups of coffee exactly how I like them to the bedtime stories when I can't sleep. More than that though, I want to thank her for being the easiest person to love, for convincing me I am too.

I also want to thank my mum, Rachel King, who navigates a different world than the one I do but has spent my life building a bridge between them. Mum, you are my North Star. To my dad, Keith Harris, we may not share blood, but you have spent my life making that small fact completely irrelevant. Loving me is a choice you make every day, and I cannot thank you enough. Thanks for the books. My brother, Lee, my forever friend and the star of my favorite childhood memories—love you, bro. My aunty, Crystal, thanks for teaching me so much about mac and cheese, LA, and myself; I hope you know that your intelligence and elegance is one of my biggest inspirations in life.

I want to thank my doctoral supervisor, Dr. Dawn-Marie Gibson, who has been editing my essays since I was a precocious eighteen-year-old. Thanks for helping me see that academia was a place for me and answering my questions for over ten years. No one has done more for my development as a thinker, so I'm forever grateful for your guidance and support (even the red underlined edits).

Authors always say in this part that writing a book takes a village, and how true that is. To the best agent a girl could ask for, Silé Edwards. Sometimes someone comes into your life, and you immediately take a breath of relief and think "there you are." Thank you for the confidence, the laughs, the edits, and for tirelessly changing this complicated industry for the better. To the most amazing editor, Maya Fernandez. Thank you for always giving me validation with the edits, for truly understanding what I was trying to do here and for making it possible. More importantly though, thanks for having such faith in my voice and for encouraging me. Everyone who has touched this book at Andrew Nurnberg and Beacon Press—you've all helped this happen, and I hope your pillows are always cold and your coffee is always strong. Book publishing is an industry fueled by love and dreams, and you all embody that entirely.

Now for my friends—yes, you're mentioned, here you are. Rey Shakespeare, your friendship is a force of nature always moving me in the right direction. You are light and the warmest of summer days, and I wish you all the love you effortlessly exude. Shane Thomas (though I haven't called you by this name in years), the best concert companion and friend. I am beyond grateful for you and the consistency and warmth of our friendship. Nyasha (Dr. Maposa), you made a city that was completely new to me feel like home and are the best co-working companion I could have asked for. I hope to give you back a fraction of what you continuously give me. Jenni Ashby, high school was worth it because it brought your beautiful soul into my life. I am endlessly proud of everything you are and all you will become. To Dr. Khaliden Nas, perhaps the first person to take my rantings about Beyoncé seriously and one of the most intelligent and elegant people I know. You once called Beyoncé a cultural archivist, and this is one of the many things you have said that has stuck with me. PS—I know you love me, really. To my poetry community, aka my safe spaces. Jake Wild-Hall and Amy Acre, who first published me; Gabriel Akamo, who I insult constantly but lovingly; and Peter De-Graft Johnson and Joel Austerson, who cemented my love of words. I adore you all endlessly; you keep me writing. And, to the best wordsmith I've ever had the pleasure of knowing, Gboyega Odubanjo—you'd have teased me so much for writing this book and for the price I paid for my COWBOY CARTER tickets. I miss you.

Thank you to the Hive. This one is truly for you. Long may we buzz, overanalyze Beyoncé's social media posts, and take fire-outfit pictures.

Last, to everyone who has had to listen to me talk about Beyoncé, you may think this book means I am done talking about her. I am not.

NOTES

Introduction

1. Cambridge Dictionary, "bootylicious," https://dictionary.cambridge.org/dictionary/english/bootylicious, accessed December 3, 2025.

2. "Beyoncé Adopts 'Fierce' Alter-Ego," BBC, October 24, 2008, http://news.bbc.co.uk/1/mobile/entertainment/7688799.stm.

3. Tim Noakes, "Beyoncé: The Simple Life," *Dazed*, July 2011, https://www.dazeddigital.com/music/article/10868/1/beyonce-the-simple-life.

4. Recording Academy, "Adele Wins Album of the Year | Acceptance Speech | 59th GRAMMYs," YouTube, February 13, 2017, https://www.youtube.com/watch?v=ctuggqUSITM.

Beyoncé, Kelly, Michelle, the Super Bowl, and Sisterhood

1. "Beyoncé," Super Bowl XLVII Halftime Show, February 3, 2013,

2. Sope Soetan, "Destiny's Child's Debut Album at 25: How a Neo-Soul Album from Teens Spawned R&B Legends," Grammy.com, February 16, 2023, https://www.grammy.com/news/revisit-destinys-child-debut-album-25th-anniversary-beyonce-knowles-no-no-no.

3. Tina Knowles, *Matriarch: A Memoir* (Dialogue Books/One World, 2025), 280.

4. Hollywood Walk of Fame, "Destiny's Child," https://walkoffame.com/destinys-child/, accessed November 3, 2025.

5. Eric Russ, "Kelly Rowland Ventures from Pop Star to Star Curator," Sotheby's, February 23, 2023, https://www.sothebys.com/en/articles/artist-actress-producer-and-now-curator-kelly-rowland-at-sothebys.

The Dreadful Irony of Women's Sexuality as Told Through Beyoncé's Discography

1. Tom Brook, "The Birth of a Nation: The Most Racist Movie Ever Made?" BBC, February 6, 2015, https://www.bbc.co.uk/culture/article/20150206-the-most-racist-movie-ever-made.

2. *Jungle Fever*, directed by Spike Lee (40 Acres and a Mule Filmworks, 1991), DVD.

3. Beyoncé, "Baby Boy (video) ft. Sean Paul," YouTube, October 3, 2009, https://www.youtube.com/watch?v=8ucz_pm3LX8.

4. Beyoncé, "Naughty Girl," YouTube, March 17, 2011, https://www.youtube.com/watch?v=RZuJ_OHBN78.

5. Beyoncé, "Get Me Bodied (Extended Mix)," YouTube, October 3, 2009, https://www.youtube.com/watch?v=RioOJ7dZxuw.

6. Beyoncé, "Freakum Dress," YouTube, October 3, 2009, https://www.youtube.com/watch?v=ArDXxTsJJoo.

7. Beyoncé, "Check On It (Official Video) ft. Bun B, Slim Thug," YouTube, October 3, 2009, https://www.youtube.com/watch?v=Q1dUDzBdnmI.

8. Beyoncé, "Ego," YouTube, October 3, 2009, https://www.youtube.com/watch?v=hbnPkK76Ask.

9. Beyoncé, "Dance for You (Video)," YouTube, November 27, 2011, https://www.youtube.com/watch?v=PGc9n6BiWXA.

10. "Beyoncé Leads Time's 100 Most Influential People," BBC, April 25, 2014, https://www.bbc.co.uk/news/entertainment-arts-27154568.

11. Montéz Jennings, "'America Has a Problem' If Beyoncé Is a Terrorist: On bell hooks Teaching Me to Think," *Compstudies*, Chapman University, July 23, 2023, https://compstudiesjournal.com/2023/07/12/america-has-a-problem-if-beyonce-is-a-terrorist-on-bell-hooks-teaching-me-to-think/.

Feminist

1. Chimamanda Ngozi Adichie, "We Should All Be Feminists," TEDx Talk, April 12, 2013, https://www.youtube.com/watch?v=hg3umXU_qWc.

2. Cambridge University Press, "feminism," https://dictionary.cambridge.org/dictionary/english/feminism, accessed November 3, 2025.

3. Eliana Dockterman, "Flawless: 5 Lessons in Modern Feminism from Beyoncé," *Time*, December 17, 2013, https://time.com/1851/flawless-5-lessons-in-modern-feminism-from-beyonce/.

4. Beyoncé, "Me, Myself and I (Video Version)," YouTube, October 3, 2009, https://www.youtube.com/watch?v=4S37SGxZSMc.

5. Beyoncé, "Diva," YouTube, October 3, 2009, https://www.youtube.com/watch?v=rNM5HW13_O8.

6. Beyoncé, "Run the World (Girls) (Official Video)," YouTube, May 18, 2011, https://www.youtube.com/watch?v=VBmMU_iwe6U.

7. Beyoncé, "Beyoncé Performs 'Run the World (Girls)' at the 2011 Billboard Music Awards," YouTube, December 15, 2011, https://www.youtube.com/watch?v=5EwZ_AzDDM4.

8. Beyoncé, "Pretty Hurts," directed by Melina Matsoukas (Parkwood Entertainment, 2013), YouTube, April 24, 2014, https://www.youtube.com/watch?v=LXXQLa-5n5w.

9. Beyoncé, "***Flawless," directed by Mark Ronson (Columbia Records, 2013), YouTube, November 24, 2014, https://www.youtube.com/watch?v=IyuUWOnS9BY.

10. Adichie, "We Should All Be Feminists."

Even People Who Don't Like Beyoncé Like "Single Ladies"

1. Beyoncé, "Single Ladies (Put a Ring on It)," directed by Jake Nava (Sony Music Entertainment, 2008), YouTube, October 3, 2009, https://www.youtube.com/watch?v=4m1EFMoRFvY.

2. Hilary Hughes, "10 Years of 'Single Ladies': Beyoncé's Director, Choreographers & More Put a Ring on Her Iconic Music Video," *Billboard*, July 26, 2018, https://www.billboard.com/music/pop/beyonce-single-ladies-put-a-ring-on-it-oral-history-8467159/.

3. Cheryl Brody Franklin, "VMA Moment: How Much Do You Love Taylor Swift and Beyoncé?" *Glamour*, September 14, 2009, https://www.glamour.com/story/vma-moment-how-much-do-you-lov.

4. Gil Kaufman, "Justin Timberlake Recalls Pitching Beyoncé on 'Single Ladies' Male Dancer 'SNL' Sketch: 'She Was Not Having It,'" *Billboard*, January 28, 2025, https://www.billboard.com/music/pop/justin-timberlake-talks-convincing-beyonce-single-ladies-male-dancer-snl-sketch-1235885679/.

5. Hughes, "10 Years of 'Single Ladies.'"

6. CNN, "Obama Reminds Guys to 'Put a Ring on It,'" YouTube, November 13, 2012, https://youtu.be/_3M5t_aaODI?si=zX6DJBQjUxDSivCN.

7. Hughes, "10 Years of 'Single Ladies.'"

An Ode to Beyoncé as an Actress

1. Laurence Mark, *Dreamgirls*, directed by Bill Condon (DreamWorks Home Entertainment, 2007).

2. Oscars, "Jennifer Hudson Wins Best Supporting Actress/79th Oscars (2007)," YouTube, October 29, 2010, https://www.youtube.com/watch?v=IvclyTi6UcA.

3. "Dreamgirls," IMDB.com, https://www.imdb.com/title/tt0443489/, accessed February 4, 2026.

4. David Sims, "Remembering Beyoncé's Career-Best Performance in 'Cadillac Records,'" *The Atlantic*, September 4, 2014, https://www.theatlantic.com/culture/2014/09/remembering-beyonces-career-best-performance-in-cadillac-records/379646/.

5. Sims, "Remembering Beyoncé's Career-Best Performance in 'Cadillac Records.'"

6. *Obsessed*, directed by Steve Shill (Rainforest Films).

7. *Cadillac Records*, directed by Darnell Martin (Sony Pictures Home Entertainment, 2008), DVD.

"Formation" and Floodwater

1. *Saturday Night Live*, "The Day Beyoncé Turned Black," YouTube, February 14, 2016, https://www.youtube.com/watch?v=ociMBfkDG1w.

2. *Saturday Night Live*, "The Day Beyoncé Turned Black."

3. Beyoncé, *Lemonade* (Parkwood Entertainment, 2016).

4. "Extremely Powerful Hurricane Katrina Leaves a Historic Mark on the Northern Gulf Coast: A Killer Hurricane Our Country Will Never Forget," National Weather Service, https://www.weather.gov/mob/katrina#:~:text=A%20Killer%20Hurricane%20Our%20Country%20Will%20Never%20Forget&text=In%20addition%2C%20Katrina%20is%20one,un%2Dadjusted%202005%20dollars, accessed February 4, 2026.

5. Barack Obama, foreword to *The State of Black America* (National Urban League, 2007), 11.

6. *Democracy Now!*, "George W. Bush Does Not Care About Black People: Reflections on Kanye West's Criticism 10 Years After," YouTube, August 28, 2015, https://www.youtube.com/watch?v=lTuRPuhneAs.

7. CNN, "Report: Criticism of FEMA's Katrina Response Deserved," April 14, 2006, https://edition.cnn.com/2006/POLITICS/04/14/fema.ig/.

8. *Democracy Now!*, "George W. Bush Does Not Care About Black People."

9. Beyoncé, "Formation," directed by Melina Matsoukas, music video, YouTube, December 9, 2016, https://www.youtube.com/watch?v=WDZJPJV__bQ.

10. Reniqua Allen and Quartz, "Why Blue Ivy's Hair Matters," *The Atlantic*, June 19, 2014, https://www.theatlantic.com/entertainment/archive/2014/06/stop-protesting-blue-ivys-hairstyle-and-celebrate-what-it-really-means/373060/; Jia Wertz, "Grown Adults Are Calling Blue Ivy Ugly on the Internet," *HuffPost UK*, September 1, 2016, updated

September 14, 2016, https://www.huffingtonpost.co.uk/entry/grownadultsarecallingblueivyuglyontheinternet_us_57c83f1ee4b06c750dd8e510.

11. Rebeca Trejo, "A Brief History of New Orleans Bounce Music Style," *Culture Trip*, July 22, 2021, https://theculturetrip.com/north-america/usa/louisiana/articles/history-of-bounce-music.

12. Rasha Ali and David Oliver, "Slang Comes from Black LGBT+ Communities," *USA Today*, June 17, 2021, https://eu.usatoday.com/in-depth/life/2021/06/17/slang-comes-from-black-lgbtq-communities-not-honoring-that-racism/7639721002/.

13. NFL, "Beyoncé & Bruno Mars Crash the Pepsi Super Bowl 50 Halftime Show," YouTube, February 11, 2016, https://www.youtube.com/watch?v=SDPITj1wlkg.

14. *Entertainment Tonight*, "Rudy Giuliani Slams Beyoncé's Black Panther Super Bowl Tribute: 'It Was Outrageous!'" YouTube, February 9, 2016, https://www.youtube.com/watch?v=X32rmKAbhHU.

15. Shay Dawson, "Sister Rosetta Tharpe," National Women's History Museum, https://www.womenshistory.org/education-resources/biographies/sister-rosetta-tharpe, accessed November 3, 2025.

16. Marissa Lorusso, "How One of Music's Biggest Stars Almost Disappeared, and How Her Legacy Was Saved," NPR, September 27, 2019, https://www.npr.org/2019/09/27/759601364/how-one-of-musics-biggest-stars-almost-disappeared-and-how-her-legacy-was-saved.

17. Malcolm X, "Who Taught You to Hate?" YouTube, September 9, 2014, https://www.youtube.com/watch?v=Re8EYUH1dD8.

18. Nakisha Lewis, "Black Women Are Tired of Being the Mule of America," *Blavity*, August 4, 2022, https://blavity.com/black-women-mule-america-fight-help-respect-justice-equity?category1=opinion.

19. "Serena Williams Sits Down with Common to Talk About Race and Identity," *Andscape*, December 19, 2016, https://andscape.com/features/serena-williams-sits-down-with-common-to-talk-about-race-and-identity/.

20. "African Origins of Twerking," *Progressive Pupil* (blog), October 26, 2013, https://progressivepupil.wordpress.com/2013/10/26/african-origins-of-twerking/.

21. Kamryn Z. Bess, "It's More Than 'Just' Hair: Revitalization of Black Identity," *Folklife Magazine*, November 7, 2022, https://folklife.si.edu/magazine/black-hair-identity.

22. Rachel Barns, "Black History Month Means Confronting My Slave Plantation Roots," NBC News, February 28, 2020, https://www.nbcnews.com/think/opinion/black-history-month-confronting-my-slave-plantation-roots-ncna1145131.

23. Beyoncé and Kendrick Lamar, "Freedom," BET Awards, Los Angeles, June 27, 2016.

24. Martin Luther King Jr., "I Have a Dream," August 1963, *American Texts*, https://www1.udel.edu/htr/American/Texts/king.html.

25. Beyoncé, "Formation."

Beychella—the University of Beyoncé

1. Carolyn Bernucca, "Beychella One Year Later," *Complex*, April 12, 2019, https://www.complex.com/music/a/carolyn-bernucca/beychella-one-year-later-making-of.

2. Alex Taylor, "The Iconography Behind Beyoncé's 'Iconic' Coachella Sets," BBC, April 23, 2018, https://www.bbc.co.uk/news/entertainment-arts-43783861.

3. Beyoncé, *Homecoming: A Film by Beyoncé*, directed by Beyoncé and Ed Burke (Netflix, 2019).

4. Jonathan Borge, "The Meaning Behind Beyoncé's Coachella Outfits in Netflix's *Homecoming*," *Oprah Daily*, April 16, 2019, https://www.oprahdaily.com/entertainment/tv-movies/a27172349/beyonce-homecoming-coachella-outfits-meaning-crest/.

5. Erica L. Green, "Why Students Are Choosing H.B.C.U.s: '4 Years Being Seen as Family,'" *New York Times*, June 11, 2022, updated June 22, 2023, https://www.nytimes.com/2022/06/11/us/hbcu-enrollment-black-students.html.

6. Jamaal Abdul-Alim, "The Untold Story of How Howard University Came to Be Known as 'The Mecca,'" *The Conversation*, September 6, 2023, https://theconversation.com/the-untold-story-of-how-howard-university-came-to-be-known-as-the-mecca-212245.

7. Green, "Why Students Are Choosing H.B.C.U.s."

8. Ta-Nehisi Coates, *Between the World and Me* (Spiegel & Grau, 2015), 39.

9. Akira Kyles, "Step Culture: 'It's Something I Think the Black Community Should Be Proud Of,'" *Fayetteville Observer*, updated April 18, 2022, https://www.fayobserver.com/story/lifestyle/2022/04/18/significance-step-culture-black-community/9510880002/?gnt-cfr=1&gca-cat=p&gca-uir=true&gca-epti=z114947d00----v114947d--55--b--55--&gca-ft=159&gca-ds=sophi.

10. Beyoncé, *Homecoming.*

11. NAACP, "Lift Every Voice and Sing," https://naacp.org/find-resources/history-explained/lift-every-voice-and-sing, accessed January 8, 2026.

12. Beyoncé, *Homecoming.*

13. Beyoncé, *Homecoming.*

14. Luvvie Ajayi, "Beychella Is Proof That Beyoncé Is the Greatest Performer Alive: I'm Not Arguing," in *Queen Bey: A Celebration of the Power and Creativity of Beyoncé Knowles-Carter*, ed. Veronica Chambers (St. Martin's, 2019), 13.

Going Global

1. Karen Cooper, "Haint Blue—a History of Porches, Evil Spirits and Paint," *Forsyth Family*, April 1, 2023, https://forsythfamilymagazine.com/haint-blue-a-history-of-porches-evil-spirits-and-paint/.

2. Katie Holdefehr, "Why So Many Southern Porches Have Blue Ceilings and How to Copy It," *Real Simple*, August 10, 2017, https://www.realsimple.com/home-organizing/decorating/tips-techniques/blue-porch-ceiling.

3. Lior Phillips, "The Lion Sleeps Tonight: One Song's Journey from 1930s South Africa to Disney Money-Spinner," *The Guardian*, May 8, 2023, https://www.theguardian.com/music/2023/may/08/mbube-the-lion-sleeps-tonight-lion-king.

4. Khalid Nas, interview with the author, February 2024.

5. Naima Mohamus, "Is Mansa Musa the Richest Man Who Ever Lived?" BBC Africa, March 9, 2019, https://www.bbc.co.uk/news/world-africa-47379458.

6. "Ranked: The World's Top Diamond Mining Countries, by Carats and Value," Mining.com, October 4, 2023, https://www.mining.com/web/ranked-the-worlds-top-diamond-mining-countries-by-carats-and-value/.

7. *Encyclopedia of African Religion*, "Ashe," Sage Knowledge, https://sk.sagepub.com/ency/edvol/africanreligion/chpt/ashe, accessed November 20, 2025.

8. Paulina Michael, "The Racial Roots Behind the Term 'Nappy,'" *Code Switch*, August 9, 2019, https://www.npr.org/sections/codeswitch/2019/08/09/412886884/the-racial-roots-behind-the-term-nappy.

9. North Northamptonshire Council, "Pan-African Flag—Black History Month," n.d., https://www.northnorthants.gov.uk/community-safety-and-emergencies/black-history-month-2022/pan-african-flag-black-history-month, accessed January 23, 2026.

10. *Beyoncé Presents: Making* The Gift, directed by Beyoncé Knowles-Carter (ABC, 2019).

11. National Museum of African American History and Culture, "The Historical Legacy of Juneteenth," https://nmaahc.si.edu/explore/stories/historical-legacy-juneteenth, accessed November 3, 2025.

12. Akili King, "Activist Tamika D. Mallory on Her Viral Speech and What True Allyship Looks Like," *Vogue*, June 6, 2020, https://www.vogue.com

/article/activist-tamika-d-mallory-on-her-viral-speech-and-what-true-allyship-looks-like.

13. Ta-Nehisi Coates, "The Case for Reparations," *The Atlantic*, June 2014, https://www.theatlantic.com/magazine/archive/2014/06/the-case-for-reparations/361631/.

14. NowThis Impact, "Marianne Williamson Defends Reparations Plan During Democratic Debate," You Tube, July 30, 2019, https://www.youtube.com/watch?v=3dztdTWMoos.

15. Henry Louis Gates Jr., "The Truth Behind '40 Acres and a Mule,'" *The African Americans: Many Rivers to Cross* (blog), PBS, January 7, 2013, https://www.pbs.org/wnet/african-americans-many-rivers-to-cross/history/the-truth-behind-40-acres-and-a-mule/.

16. Terry Gross, "Historian Eric Foner on the Unresolved Legacy of Reconstruction," NPR, June 5, 2020, https://www.npr.org/2020/06/05/870459750/historian-eric-foner-on-the-unresolved-legacy-of-reconstruction.

17. Ana Monroy Yglesias, "Beyoncé Celebrates Juneteenth with 'Black Parade' & Epic Black-Owned Businesses Directory," Grammy Awards, June 22, 2020, https://www.grammy.com/news/beyonce-celebrates-juneteenth-black-parade-epic-black-owned-businesses-directory.

18. Judicaelle Irakoze, "Why We Must Be Careful When Watching Beyoncé's 'Black Is King,'" *Essence*, November 4, 2020, https://www.essence.com/entertainment/only-essence/beyonces-black-is-king-criticism/.

19. Candace McDuffie, "Beyoncé's *Black Is King* Is Exactly What We Need Right Now," *Glamour*, July 31, 2020, https://www.glamour.com/story/beyonce-black-is-king-review.

Beyoncé as a Soundtrack to Heartbreak and Healing

1. Cary Franklin, "Separate Spheres," *Yale Law Journal* 123, no. 8 (2014): 2878–2905, http://www.jstor.org/stable/43617009.

2. Daphne Brooks, *Liner Notes for the Revolution: The Intellectual Life of Black Feminist Sound* (Harvard University Press, 2021), 445.

3. Noah Yoo, "Beyoncé and JAY-Z Sued by Jamaican Artist Sampled on 'Black Effect,'" https://pitchfork.com/news/beyonce-and-jay-z-sued-by-jamaican-artist-sampled-on-black-effect/, accessed February 9, 2026.

4. Jaelani Turner Williams, "5 Facts to Know About Exploited 19th-Century Attraction Sarah Baartman," BET, April 1, 2025, https://www.bet.com/article/7envms/5-facts-to-know-about-exploited-19th-century-attraction-sarah-baartman.

5. Brittney Cooper, "Jay-Z's Apology to Beyoncé Isn't Just Celebrity Gossip—It's a Political Act," in *Queen Bey: A Celebration of the Power and Creativity of Beyoncé Knowles-Carter*, ed. Veronica Chambers (St. Martin's, 2019), 30.

6. The Carters, "APESHIT (Official Video)," YouTube, June 16, 2018, https://www.youtube.com/watch?v=kbMqWXnpXcA.

7. Maria Brito, "The Art of Being Beyoncé," in Chambers, *Queen Bey*, 57.

Eight Reasons Why I Cried at the RENAISSANCE World Tour

1. Stufish, "Beyoncé—Renaissance," 2023, https://stufish.com/project/beyonce/.

2. "Beyoncé Dedicates GLAAD Award to Gay Uncle Who Died from HIV," BBC, March 29, 2019, https://www.bbc.co.uk/news/newsbeat-47745901.

3. Bianca Betancourt, "Beyoncé Says *Renaissance* Is Dedicated to Her Family and Queer Fan Base," *Harper's Bazaar*, July 28, 2022, https://www.harpersbazaar.com/culture/art-books-music/a40742856/beyonce-dedicates-renaissance-to-queer-fans/.

4. "Beyoncé Speaks Out Against Racism and Sexism in Graduation Speech," BBC News, June 8, 2020, https://www.bbc.co.uk/news/entertainment-arts-52962717.

5. Beyoncé, "7/11," directed by Beyoncé (Parkwood Entertainment and Columbia Records, 2013), YouTube, November 21, 2014, https://www.youtube.com/watch?v=k4YRWT_Aldo.

6. Taiyler S. Mitchell, "Once Again, Beyoncé Says 'You Are the Visual, Baby,'" *Huffington Post UK*, November 9, 2024, https://www.huffingtonpost.co.uk/entry/beyonce-visual-renaissance-album_n_66e097d4e4b0278730821f0e.

7. José Criales-Unzueta, "Beyoncé's *Renaissance* Tour Outfits from the Runway to the Concert Arena—and Now to the Big Screen," *Vogue*, November 27, 2023, https://www.vogue.com/article/beyonce-renaissance-looks-from-the-runway.

8. Kaitlyn Greenidge, "Beyoncé's Evolution," *Harper's Bazaar*, August 10, 2021, https://www.harpersbazaar.com/culture/features/a37039502/beyonce-evolution-interview-2021/.

9. Maria Brito, "The Art of Being Beyoncé," *Queen Bey: A Celebration of the Power and Creativity of Beyoncé Knowles-Carter*, ed. Veronica Chambers (St. Martin's, 2019), 53.

10. *Renaissance: A Film by Beyoncé*, directed by Beyoncé (Parkwood Entertainment, 2023).

An Ode to the Contradiction of "CHURCH GIRL" and the Beauty of Voodoo

1. *Entertainment Tonight*, "Beyoncé Calls Gospel Most POWERFUL Type of Music (Flashback)," YouTube, September 24, 2023, https://www.youtube.com/watch?v=uqVqqV0DBp4.

2. Destiny's Child, "Survivor (Official Video)," YouTube, October 25, 2009, https://www.youtube.com/watch?v=Wmc8bQoL-J0.

3. Laënnec Hurbon, "Haitian Vodou," in *The Open Encyclopedia of Anthropology*, ed. Felix Stein, initially published April 5, 2022, facsimile of the first edition in *The Cambridge Encyclopedia of Anthropology*, http://doi.org/10.29164/22haitianvodou.

4. Michelle Y. Gordon, "'Midnight Scenes and Orgies': Public Narratives of Voodoo in New Orleans and Nineteenth-Century Discourses of White Supremacy," *American Quarterly* 64, no. 4 (2012): 767–86, http://www.jstor.org/stable/41809523.

Black Motherhood as Performance and Politics

1. "The 59th Annual Grammy Awards," February 12, 2017, Los Angeles.

2. Tyler Mitchell, "Beyoncé in Her Own Words: Her Life, Her Body, Her Heritage," *Vogue*, August 6, 2018, https://www.vogue.com/article/beyonce-september-issue-2018.

3. Serena Williams, "What My Life-Threatening Experience Taught Me About Giving Birth," CNN, February 20, 2018, https://edition.cnn.com/2018/02/20/opinions/protect-mother-pregnancy-williams-opinion/index.html.

4. Christopher J. P. Sewell, "Mammies and Matriarchs: Tracing Images of the Black Female in Popular Culture 1950s to Present," *Journal of African American Studies* 17, no. 3 (2013): 308–26, http://www.jstor.org/stable/43526418.

5. bell hooks, *Reel to Real: Race, Class and Sex at the Movies* (Routledge, 2009).

6. Beyoncé, *Homecoming: A Film by Beyoncé*, directed by Beyoncé and Ed Burke (Netflix, 2019).

7. Beyoncé, "Blue," track 14, *Beyoncé* (Parkwood Entertainment and Columbia Records, 2013).

Beyoncé, Football, a Christmas Funeral, My Grandma, and Legacy

1. Jacqueline Whiting Bostic, "A Family Story: Juneteenth and the Founding of Emancipation Park," Voices of the Civil Rights Movement, https://voicesofthecivilrightsmovement.com/articles/juneteenth-2023, accessed May 18, 2025.

2. Compton Cowboys homepage, https://comptoncowboys.com/, accessed May 26, 2025.

3. Josh Toussaint-Strauss, "Why the First US Cowboys Were Black," *The Guardian*, October 29, 2020, video, https://www.theguardian.com/culture/video/2020/oct/29/why-the-first-us-cowboys-were-black.

4. Katie Nodjimbadem, "The Lesser-Known History of

African-American Cowboys," *Smithsonian Magazine*, February 13, 2017, https://www.smithsonianmag.com/history/lesser-known-history-african-american-cowboys-180962144/.

5. Bill Pickett Invitational Rodeo, https://www.billpickettrodeo.com/, accessed November 15, 2025.

6. Matthew Wills, "Black Cowboys and the History of the Rodeo," *JSTOR Daily*, February 11, 2021, https://daily.jstor.org/black-cowboys-and-the-history-of-the-rodeo/.

7. Lisi Niesner, "The Majestic Lipizzaner," Reuters, April 26, 2012, https://www.reuters.com/article/world/the-majestic-lipizzaner-idUS2387625397/.

8. Larisha Paul, "Shaboozey Deserves More Than What the CMA Awards Gave Him—Including an Apology," *Rolling Stone*, November 21, 2024, https://www.rollingstone.com/music/music-country/shaboozey-cma-awards-controversy-1235174910/.

9. Cynthia Littleton, "Netflix Christmas Day NFL Games Average 24 Million Viewers in U.S.," *Variety*, December 26, 2024, https://variety.com/2024/biz/news/netflix-christmas-day-nfl-games-beyonce-1236260289/.

"The Mic Is On"—the Power and Elevation of Beyoncé's Live Performances

1. *Rolling Stone*, "The 70 Greatest Beyoncé Songs," April 1, 2024, https://www.rollingstone.com/music/music-lists/best-beyonce-songs-1378620/.

2. Luvvie Ajayi, "Beychella Is Proof That Beyoncé Is the Greatest Performer Alive: I'm Not Arguing," in *Queen Bey: A Celebration of the Power and Creativity of Beyoncé Knowles-Carter*, ed. Veronica Chambers (St. Martin's, 2019), 17.

3. Beyoncé, "Listen (Live at Oprah, 2006)," YouTube, 5:16, posted by Camilla Tribe, March 24, 2013, https://www.youtube.com/watch?v=pai1C2dsd3M.

4. Beyoncé, "Ring the Alarm" performance, MTV Video Music Awards, Radio City Music Hall, New York, August 31, 2006.

5. Jordan Zakarin, "Beyoncé Sings National Anthem at Super Bowl Press Conference, Explains Lip Syncing," *Hollywood Reporter*, January 31, 2013, https://www.hollywoodreporter.com/music/music-news/beyonce-sings-national-anthem-at-417235/.

6. Beyoncé, "If I Were a Boy (Grammys on CBS)," YouTube, February 2, 2010, https://www.youtube.com/watch?v=UqzKEMqKwf0.

7. Billboard Staff, "Beyoncé's BBMA Performance: 'I Never Worked So Hard in My Life,'" *Billboard*, May 25, 2011, https://www.billboard.com/music/music-news/beyonces-bbma-performance-i-never-worked-so-hard-in-my-life-471200/.

8. Alicia Adejobi, "Beyoncé Headlined Glastonbury 10 Years Ago Today—and Changed the Festival Forever," *Metro*, June 30, 2021, https://metro.co.uk/2021/06/26/beyonce-fans-mark-10th-anniversary-of-glastonbury-performance-14825836/.

9. "Beyoncé Live at Glastonbury," BBC, 2011, https://www.bbc.co.uk/events/eg49mb/play/a358q9/p00j280x.

10. Lauren Schutte, "Beyoncé's Baby Announcement Breaks Twitter Record," *Hollywood Reporter*, August 29, 2011, https://www.hollywoodreporter.com/news/music-news/beyonces-baby-announcement-breaks-twitter-228981/.

11. Beyoncé, "Super Bowl XLVII Halftime Show," Mercedes-Benz Superdome, New Orleans, February 3, 2013.

12. Claire Anderson, "Empowerment, Agency, and Nuance at the 2013 Super Bowl Halftime Show," *Ethnomusicology Review* 19 (2014). https://ethnomusicologyreview.ucla.edu/journal/volume/19/piece/798.

13. "VMA Show-Stopper: Beyoncé Reigns as Queen of the MTV Video Music Awards," *The Guardian*, August 25, 2014, https://www.theguardian.com/culture/2014/aug/25/vma-show-stopper-beyonce-reigns-queen-mtv-video-music-awards.

14. Beyoncé, "Beyoncé—Made in America 2015 (Live Concert)," YouTube, October 11, 2024, https://www.youtube.com/watch?v=jUTLKzrzwuE.

15. Hermione Hoby, "Beyoncé: Formation Tour Review—Defiant, Victorious and Glorious," *The Guardian*, April 28, 2016.

16. Beyoncé, "Love Drought/Sandcastles." Performance at the 59th Annual Grammy Awards, Staples Center, Los Angeles, February 12, 2017.

17. Beyoncé. *Homecoming: A Film by Beyoncé*, directed by Beyoncé and Ed Burke (Netflix, 2019).

18. Molly Saxby, "Beyoncé's Live Performance Evolution 1999–2005," *Seat Unique*, February 14, 2005, https://www.seatunique.com/blog/beyonce-live-performance-evolution/.

19. Kevin O'Keeffe, "An Abbreviated History of Beyoncé Lip-Synching and Breaking Our Hearts," *The Atlantic*, September 16, 2014, https://www.theatlantic.com/culture/archive/2014/09/an-abbreviated-history-of-beyonce-lip-synching-and-breaking-our-hearts/380310/.

20. xaandde, "You Can't Put Blue Lights On Black Girls!" YouTube, 11:24, uploaded November 16, 2012, https://www.youtube.com/watch?v=MEcvP2llaCw.

21. *Renaissance: A Film by Beyoncé*, directed by Beyoncé (Parkwood Entertainment, 2023).

Changing the Game—Beyoncé's Continued Impact on the Industry

1. iHeartRadio, "Beyoncé Accepts the Innovator Award at the 2024 iHeartRadio Music Awards," YouTube, April 2, 2004, https://www.youtube.com/watch?v=a—C9lyvq-k.

2. Sughnen Yongo, "Want a Long-Lasting Career? 3 Lessons Beyoncé Can Teach You," *Forbes*, November 11, 2024, https://www.forbes.com/sites/sughnenyongo/2024/11/11/want-a-long-lasting-career-3-lessons-beyonc-can-teach-you/.

3. Michael Eric Dyson, "Beyoncé. Amen," *New York Times*, December 3, 2023, https://www.nytimes.com/2023/12/03/opinion/beyonce-renaissance-religion.html.

4. Cady Lang, "How Beyoncé Changed the Music Industry," *Time*, March 28, 2024, https://time.com/6961069/beyonce-music-industry/.

5. Beyoncé, *Beyoncé: Life Is but a Dream*, directed by Beyoncé and Ed Burke (Parkwood Entertainment and Columbia Records, 2013).

6. Spencer Kornhaber, "Beyoncé's 'Flawless': The Full Story," *The Atlantic*, June 26, 2014, https://www.theatlantic.com/entertainment/archive/2014/06/the-full-story-of-beyonces-flawless/373480/.

7. Michael Eric Dyson, "The King of Pop and the Queen of Everything," in *Queen Bey: A Celebration of the Power and Creativity of Beyoncé Knowles-Carter*, ed. Veronica Chambers (St. Martin's, 2019), 117.

8. Frankiefrankiefrank, "10 Years Ago, Beyoncé Released Her Self-Titled Album," r/popheads, Reddit, https://www.reddit.com/r/popheads/comments/18gwxnk/10_years_ago_beyonc%C3%A9_released_her_selftitled_album/, accessed December 3, 2025.

9. Edward Enninful, "B Ready: Beyoncé Is Poised for Her Next Evolution," *Vogue*, July 2022, https://www.vogue.co.uk/fashion/article/beyonce-vogue-cover-new-music.

10. Gary Trust, "'Cuff It' Becomes Beyoncé's Longest-Charting Solo Hot 100 Hit," *Billboard*, November 4, 2023, https://www.billboard.com/music/chart-beat/beyonce-cuff-it-longest-charting-solo-hot-100-hit-1235301067/.

11. Rachel Shin, "Yelp Coins the 'Beyoncé Bump' for the Economic Halo Created by the Pop Star's Renaissance Tour," *Fortune*, July 19, 2023, https://fortune.com/2023/07/19/beyonce-renaissance-tour-economic-impact/.

12. Ashlee Marie Preston, "How Beyoncé's Reinventions Are Redefining Global Travel and Tourism," *Forbes*, January 3, 2025.

13. Laura Snapes, "The Chicks: 'We Were Used and Abused by Everybody Who Wanted to Make Money Off Us,'" *The Guardian*, July 18, 2020, https://www.theguardian.com/music/2020/jul/18/dixie-chicks-used-and-abused-by-everybody-who-wanted-to-make-money-off-us.

14. David Browne, "Linda Martell, Country's Lost Pioneer," *Rolling Stone*, September 2, 2020, https://www.rollingstone.com/music/music-features/linda-martell-black-country-grand-ole-opry-pioneer-1050432/.

15. Tamara Palmer, "Beyoncé Is the Genre-Bending Queen on 'Cowboy Carter': 5 Takeaways from Her New Album," Grammy.com, March 29, 2024, https://www.grammy.com/news/beyonce-cowboy-carter-review-new-album-takeaways-country.

16. Shelby Stewart, "Beyoncé Accepts Innovator Award at 2024 iHeartRadio Music Awards," *Essence*, April 2, 2024, https://www.essence.com/entertainment/beyonce-receives-innovator-award-2024-iheartradio-music-awards/?utm_source=chatgpt.com.

17. Sughnen Yongo, "What Beyoncé's Renaissance World Tour Says About the Economic Impact of Black Women," *Forbes*, October 2, 2023, https://www.forbes.com/sites/sughnenyongo/2023/10/02/what-beyoncs-renaissance-world-tour-said-about-the-economic-impact-of-black-women/.

"Beyoncé?!"—the Celebrity's Celebrity

1. CalyBryt, "Beyoncé's Gets Jay-Z from Tyra Banks," YouTube, February 18, 2009, https://www.youtube.com/watch?v=Fz4rHbrZNe8.

2. *Beyoncé: Life Is but a Dream*, directed by Beyoncé and Ed Burke (Parkwood Entertainment and Columbia Records, 2013).

3. Alessandra Stanley, "Another Cog in the Machinery of Divahood," *New York Times*, February 14, 2013, https://www.nytimes.com/2013/02/15/arts/television/beyonces-documentary-life-is-but-a-dream-on-hbo.html.

4. *I Am… Tour*, directed by Justin LeBlanc (Warner Bros., 2013), DVD.

5. Beyoncé, "Beyoncé—Year of 4," YouTube, July 1, 2011, https://www.youtube.com/watch?v=3vXXiku0580.

6. Spotify, "The Story Behind Trevor Noah Talking to Beyoncé at the GRAMMYs and How She Saved His Hair," YouTube, February 9, 2024, https://www.youtube.com/watch?v=KkRHeGd3E_4.

7. Michelle Obama (@michelleobama), "@beyonce you are a record breaker," Instagram, April 2, 2024, https://www.instagram.com/michelleobama/p/C5RYHS9u9cN/?hl=en.

8. Taylor Crumpton, "What Beyoncé's Snub at the CMAs Says About Country Music's Dangerous Hierarchy," *Time*, September 10, 2024, https://time.com/7019535/beyonce-cma-snub-essay/.

The Innovation of Beyoncé's Dictionary

1. Ashlee Marie Preston, "How Beyoncé's Reinventions Are Redefining Global Travel and Tourism," *Forbes*, January 3, 2025.

2. Cambridge Dictionary, "bootylicious," https://dictionary.cambridge.org/dictionary/english/bootylicious.

3. Zak Cheney-Rice, "8 Things in Destiny's Child's 'Bug a Boo' That Just Aren't Things Anymore," *Mic*, March 20, 2013.

4. Cara Kelly, "What Does Becky Mean? Here's the History Behind Beyoncé's 'Lemonade' Lyric That Sparked a Firestorm," *USA Today*, April 27, 2016.

5. Kelly, "What Does Becky Mean?"

Nine Reasons Why I Cried at the COWBOY CARTER Tour

1. Paul Grimstad, "Rewinding Jimi Hendrix's National Anthem," *New Yorker*, January 26, 2021, https://www.newyorker.com/culture/cultural-comment/rewinding-jimi-hendrixs-national-anthem.

2. Steven J. Horowitz, "Beyoncé Planned 'Cowboy Carter' Release Before 'Renaissance,' but 'There Was Too Much Heaviness in the World,'" *Variety*, March 29, 2024, https://variety.com/2024/music/news/beyonce-planned-cowboy-carter-release-before-renaissance-switched-1235955728/.

3. COWBOY CARTER Tour, performed by Beyoncé, various locations, 2024–2025.

Conclusion

1. Veronica Chambers, introduction to *Queen Bey: A Celebration of the Power and Creativity of Beyoncé Knowles-Carter*, ed. Veronica Chambers (St. Martin's, 2019), 3.